Virtue in Virtual Spaces

ENACTING CATHOLIC SOCIAL TRADITION

Virtue in Virtual Spaces

Catholic Social Teaching and Technology

Louisa Conwill,
Megan Levis,
and
Walter Scheirer

LITURGICAL PRESS
Collegeville, Minnesota

litpress.org

Library of Congress Cataloging-in-Publication Data

Names: Conwill, Louisa, author.
Title: Virtue in virtual spaces : Catholic social teaching and technology / Louisa Conwill, Megan Levis, and Walter Scheirer.
Description: Collegeville, Minnesota : Liturgical Press, [2024] | Series: Enacting Catholic social tradition | Includes bibliographical references. | Summary: "In this book, readers will engage with the philosophies behind their favorite social media platforms, examine how the design features in these platforms shape habits and imagination, and gain dialogue-based skills to bring virtue back into virtual spaces. The authors draw from writing on virtue ethics and Catholic Social Teaching to demonstrate the potential goodness of technology. Eight of the main themes of Catholic Social Teaching are used to build a framework for designing technology to promote human flourishing"— Provided by publisher.
Identifiers: LCCN 2024012877 (print) | LCCN 2024012878 (ebook) | ISBN 9798400800269 (trade paperback) | ISBN 9798400800276 (epub) | ISBN 9798400801402 (pdf)
Subjects: LCSH: Technology—Religious aspects—Christianity. | Social media. | Christian sociology—Catholic Church. | BISAC: RELIGION / Christian Living / Social Issues | RELIGION / Christian Theology / Ethics
Classification: LCC BR115.T42 C667 2024 (print) | LCC BR115.T42 (ebook) | DDC 261.5/6—dc23/eng/20240520
LC record available at https://lccn.loc.gov/2024012877
LC ebook record available at https://lccn.loc.gov/2024012878

To

Current patron saints of the Internet,
the late Blessed Carlo Acutis and Marshall McLuhan
and
Any and all future patron saints of the Internet

Contents

Preface   ix

Glossary of Terms   xiii

Chapter One
  Introduction   1

Chapter Two
  Historical Background of Catholic Social Teaching   22

Chapter Three
  Dialogue and Social Technologies   35

Chapter Four
  A Framework for Technology Design
  Based on Catholic Social Teaching   51

Chapter Five
  Case Studies   76

Chapter Six
  Conclusion   104

Bibliography   111

Preface

Pope Francis is the first pope to directly confront a world with universal Internet connectivity—a landmark achievement in technological progress that has dramatically reshaped society. In a speech given at the 2014 World Communications Day, he expressed sincere optimism about where things were heading with respect to technologies that allowed people from all over the globe to communicate with one another:

> The media can help us to feel closer to one another, creating a sense of the unity of the human family which in turn can inspire solidarity and serious efforts to ensure a more dignified life for all. . . . The internet, in particular, offers immense possibilities for encounter and solidarity. This is something truly good, a gift from God.[1]

But by the beginning of 2020, discourse on the Internet had taken a darker turn, dividing society in vicious new ways that made us feel farther apart rather than closer together—completely undermining the true potential of the technology. Recognizing this, Francis issued a call in his encyclical *Fratelli Tutti* to place such technologies in the service of human flourishing:

---

[1] Pope Francis, "Message for the 2014 World Communications Day (January 24, 2014)," *AAS* 106 (2014): 113.

> We need constantly to ensure that present-day forms of com-
> munication are in fact guiding us to generous encounter with
> others, to honest pursuit of the whole truth, to service, to
> closeness to the underprivileged and to the promotion of the
> common good. (205)

For technologists interested in responding to this call, the question
has been how exactly to do this.

This book is the outgrowth of a research project from a working
group at the University of Notre Dame to develop a framework
based on Catholic Social Teaching within the Catholic Social Tradition that takes up the call of Francis. It provides a socially constructive way to think about, build, and use technology in a manner that
emphasizes our shared humanity. It is based on our experiences as
professional software developers, technology ethicists, and users
of the Internet. Such a project fills a conspicuous gap in the area of
software engineering where human flourishing and the common
good are deemphasized or are entirely neglected in favor of the
creation of products that make money for the few at the expense
of the many.

This project was based at the Center for Social Concerns at the
University of Notre Dame. We want to thank all of our colleagues
and conversation partners at the Center, in particular Suzanne
Shanahan, Bill Purcell, Margie Pfeil, Dan Graff, and Connie Mick.
We also want to thank our colleagues and conversation partners
in Notre Dame's Department of Computer Science and Engineering, in particular David Chiang and Karla Badillo-Urquiola. Special recognition goes to Brett Robinson from the McGrath Institute
for Church Life at Notre Dame for his thoughts on Marshall
McLuhan and for buying us delicious scones in the final push to
complete the manuscript for this book. We also want to extend
our gratitude to Paul Blaschko from Notre Dame's Department of
Philosophy for his dialogue resources, infectious energy, and conversations about work, life, and everything in between.

Our expectation for this book is that it will be a practical tool for designers, developers, and ordinary users of digital technologies. Like Francis, we see the powerful potential for good in the Internet and hope that this book will help bring it about.

Louisa Conwill, Megan Levis, and Walter Scheirer
South Bend, Indiana
Winter 2024

Glossary of Terms

Attention Economy: a business strategy that involves applications designed in an addictive way to capture the attention of users to show them more advertising to make more money (chaps. 1, 2).

Catholic Social Teaching: the body of work in the Catholic Social Tradition addressing the human person's place in modern society, which respects the rights associated with the notion of human dignity (chaps. 1, 2, 4).

Common Good: the complete set of social conditions that provide communities and their individual members a path to follow to readily achieve fulfillment (chaps. 1, 2).

Dialogue: two or more people engaging deeply with an idea together, building off of one another to more deeply uncover the truth (chaps. 1, 3).

Generative Artificial Intelligence: algorithms capable of producing new text, images, audio, and other forms of data (chaps. 1, 6).

Human-Computer Interaction (HCI): a human-centered approach to computing, emphasizing design choices that enhance the experience of a person using a computer in novel ways (chap. 1).

Influencer: a digital creator who has amassed a large following and promotes particular lifestyles, social causes, or consumer products (chap. 4).

Open-Source Software: software that comes bundled with its source code so users, by modifying the original code, can customize a program to their liking (chap. 4).

Social Technology: any technology that facilitates social interactions or enables communication, including email, texting, video calling, and social media, among other applications (chap. 1).

Software Design Principles: guiding rules that help software developers create programs that are organized, efficient, and easy to understand (chaps. 1, 4).

Technocratic Paradigm: a mindset that views everything as a problem to be solved with science and technology (chap. 2).

Virtue Ethics: a philosophical tradition that holds that a moral agent's virtue or character is more fundamental in examining ethical issues than any specific moral rules or principles (chap. 1).

Chapter ONE

Introduction

The twenty-first century is characterized by its relentless production and deployment of new digital technologies—so much so that a great deal of life is now organized around the Internet, a global information network of unparalleled reach and scope. This is because the Internet, at its foundation, is a *social technology*. A social technology is any technology that facilitates social interactions or enables communication, including email, texting, video calling, and social media, among other applications. Social technologies have radically changed the way we communicate with and relate to others. No longer limited to the speed of a letter through the postal service, we are able to instantly message anyone in the world at any time. No longer limited to the people we cross paths with in the physical world, we are now able to share our lives through social media with people we've never met in person. Social technologies have provided us with a number of benefits: the ability to easily coordinate plans with people we regularly see, the ability to keep in touch with family and friends who live far from us, and the ability to find community in people we may otherwise have never met. The popularity of the Internet is undoubtedly connected to the inherent joy in serendipitous encounters with strangers (Matt 25:35).

At its best, the Internet channels the world into a global village of sorts, where digital citizens learn from one another, explore new modes of creation, and help others work through dilemmas in both physical and virtual spaces. And this hints at what the Internet was originally meant to be: a global network with strong communal and even spiritual dimensions. Remarkably, the Internet was in part the product of the Christian mind. One can trace its origin as a social space to the thinking of the famed media theorist and devout Catholic Marshall McLuhan.[1] Paralleling the institution of the Catholic Church, McLuhan vigorously promoted the idea of a global information network that would be a singular unifying force bringing all of humanity into a digital communion. Writing in 1961, McLuhan had this to say about why such a network would be socially constructive in his essay "The Electric Culture": "The electric movement of information abolishes the walls and boundaries between subject matters as much as between night and day and nationalities. The tribalism will consist of one tribe in one global village—to wit, the human family."[2]

Silicon Valley moved to implement McLuhan's thinking in the 1990s at the dawn of the dotcom era, which ensured the success of the Internet—its social dimension would prove to be its most enduring asset as a technology. In its inaugural issue, *WIRED* magazine dubbed McLuhan the "Patron Saint of the Internet" and introduced his ideas to a new generation of programmers who enthusiastically constructed something meant to resemble the global village: social media. Kevin Kelly, the founding executive editor of *WIRED* and a practicing Christian, believed that the act of a programmer creating a wholly new digital environment was akin to a "vision of the unbounded God binding himself to his creation."[3] This new form of creation was enabled by the capacious-

---

[1] Nick Ripatrazone, *Digital Communion: Marshall McLuhan's Spiritual Vision for a Virtual Age* (Minneapolis: Augsburg Fortress, 2022).

[2] Marshall McLuhan, "The Electric Culture," *Renascence* 13, no. 4 (November 1, 1961): 219–20.

[3] Katelyn Beatey, "Geek Theologian Kevin Kelly," *Christianity Today*, July 15, 2011, https://www.christianitytoday.com/ct/2011/julyweb-only/geektheologian.html.

ness of computer programs and the endless reach of information networks—things not typically associated with spirituality. In a recent interview with the blogger Noah Smith, Kelly characterized his long-standing belief in the inherent goodness of technology as a progressive mode of creation: "Our technologies are ultimately not contrary to life, but are in fact an extension of life, enabling it to develop yet more options and possibilities at a faster rate. Increasing options and possibilities is also known as progress . . ."[4]

So much promise can be seen in these early ideas. So what happened? As any user of today's Internet can attest, the social media experience is a frustrating, alienating, and frequently degrading affair. From relentless partisan political arguments to the deluges of shockingly vulgar content, the dominant social media platforms have become cultural wastelands where one struggles to find an oasis of friendly conversation. This is far from where McLuhan and Kelly envisioned we would be at our current state of technological development, for "the fruit of the Spirit is love, joy, peace, patience, kindness, generosity, faithfulness, gentleness, and self-control" (Gal 5:22-23)—virtues that would be needed to foster healthy communities on the Internet. To begin to develop an understanding of this situation, let's review some recent Catholic and secular thinking on social technology. Surprisingly, there is much agreement between disparate camps on where things went wrong and where there is still hope for a more virtuous Internet.

The Good and the Bad of Social Technologies

Technology has tremendous potential for good because of the inherent goodness of human creation. As the philosopher Martin Heidegger points out in his essay "The Question Concerning Technology," the word *technology* stems from the Greek word *technē*,

---

[4] Noah Smith, "Interview: Kevin Kelly, Editor, Author, and Futurist," *Noahpinion* (blog), March 7, 2023, https://www.noahpinion.blog/p/interview-kevin-kelly-editor-author.

which signifies the notion of a bringing forth—something creative, and even poetic.[5] From a Christian perspective, human creativity comes from being made in the image and likeness of God, who created the universe and everything in it. As humans, we receive a unique call to co-create with God,[6] for "we are what he has made us, created in Christ Jesus for good works, which God prepared beforehand to be our way of life" (Eph 2:10).

However, our creations are not always beautiful, especially if they are not motivated by a pursuit of truth, beauty, and goodness. Though often criticized for their alienating effects, social technologies found on the Internet have the potential to be good in and of themselves by virtue of their creation by humans. In his encyclical *Laudato Si'*, Pope Francis affirms the potential goodness of technology, stating that "technoscience, when well directed, can produce important means of improving the quality of human life, from useful domestic appliances to great transportation systems, bridges, buildings and public spaces" (103).

This is not a uniquely Christian viewpoint. Philosopher of emerging science and technology Shannon Vallor, who writes from a nonreligious perspective, tells us that "to be antitechnology is in some sense to be antihuman, for we are what we do and make, and humans have always engineered our worlds as mirrors of our distinctive needs, desires, values, and beliefs."[7] If one believes in the goodness of humanity, then one can believe in the potential goodness of technology.

Even in the midst of all the problems (which we will get to shortly), there is still optimism that technology can be built in a positive way. When discussing addictive social technologies in her book *Technology and the Virtues*, Vallor asks, "Why must we

[5] Martin Heidegger and William Lovitt, *The Question Concerning Technology* (New York: Harper & Row, 1977).

[6] Elio Sgreccia, *Personalist Bioethics: Foundations and Applications* (Philadelphia: National Catholic Bioethics Center, 2012).

[7] Shannon Vallor, *Technology and the Virtues: A Philosophical Guide to a Future Worth Wanting* (New York: Oxford University Press, 2016).

choose between debilitating tools, and digital lockboxes to keep us away from them? Why not demand useful tools that do not debilitate us?"[8] In asking these questions, Vallor is proposing that we can uncompromisingly demand that our technology serve us, not the other way around.

The three most recent popes have expressed specific hope for social technologies in response to the growing importance of the Internet in everyone's life. Pope John Paul II hoped for the Internet to be used as a tool for evangelization, declaring it "a new forum for proclaiming the Gospel"[9] and saying, "Modern technology places at our disposal unprecedented possibilities for good, for spreading the truth of our salvation in Jesus Christ and for fostering harmony and reconciliation."[10] Pope Benedict XVI expressed hope in the potential for social networks to foster healthy discussion and debate[11] and to unite the isolated.[12] Francis has highlighted the Internet's potential to foster solidarity with our global human family. In a video message to a TED conference in 2017, Francis said, "How wonderful it would be if the growth of scientific and technological innovation could come with more equality and

[8] Vallor, *Technology and the Virtues*, 169.

[9] Pope John Paul II, "36th World Communications Day—Internet: A New Forum for Proclaiming the Gospel," May 12, 2002, https://www.vatican.va /content/john-paul-ii/en/messages/communications/documents/hf_jp-ii_mes _20020122_world-communications-day.html.

[10] Pope John Paul II, "39th World Communications Day—The Communications Media: At the Service of Understanding among Peoples," May 8, 2005, https://www.vatican.va/content/john-paul-ii/en/messages/communications/ documents/hf_jp-ii_mes_20050124_world-communications-day.html.

[11] Pope Benedict XVI, "43rd World Communications Day—New Technologies, New Relationships. Promoting a Culture of Respect, Dialogue and Friendship," May 24, 2009, https://www.vatican.va/content/benedict-xvi/en /messages/communications/documents/hf_ben-xvi_mes_20090124_43rd -world-communications-day.html.

[12] Pope Benedict XVI, "47th World Communications Day—Social Networks: Portals of Truth and Faith; New Spaces for Evangelization," May 12, 2013, https:// www.vatican.va/content/benedict-xvi/en/messages/communications/documents /hf_ben-xvi_mes_20130124_47th-world-communications-day.html.

social inclusion. How wonderful would it be, even as we discover faraway planets, to rediscover the needs of the brothers and sisters who orbit around us."[13] At the 48th World Communications Day, Francis said, "The internet, in particular, offers immense possibilities for encounter and solidarity. This is something truly good, a gift from God."[14]

Of course, the popes describe a vision of an Internet that we should have, not the one we presently confront, which contains both great possibility *and* serious trouble. It is not very difficult to compile a list of social problems stemming from the conduct of businesses that control the Internet's infrastructure. Such a list would include social alienation,[15] technology addiction,[16] misinformation,[17] trolling,[18] misogyny,[19] racism and bigotry,[20] disrespectful discourse,[21] pervasive corporate surveillance,[22] and

---

[13] Pope Francis, "Video Message to the TED Conference in Vancouver," *L'Osservatore Romano* (April 26, 2017): 7.

[14] Pope Francis, "Message for the 2014 World Communications Day," 113.

[15] Jonathan Haidt, "The Teen Mental Illness Epidemic Began Around 2012," Persuasion, February 8, 2023, https://www.persuasion.community/p/haidt-the-teen-mental-illness-epidemic.

[16] Tania Moretta and Giulia Buodo, "The Relationship between Affective and Obsessive-Compulsive Symptoms in Internet Use Disorder," *Frontiers in Psychology* 12 (2021): 700518, https://doi.org/10.3389/fpsyg.2021.700518.

[17] Bobby Chesney and Danielle Citron, "Deep Fakes: A Looming Challenge for Privacy, Democracy, and National Security," *California Law Review* 107 (2019): 1753.

[18] Adrienne LaFrance, "Trolls Are Winning the Internet, Technologists Say," *The Atlantic*, March 29, 2017, https://www.theatlantic.com/technology/archive/2017/03/guys-its-time-for-some-troll-theory/521046/.

[19] Peter C. Baker, "Hunting the Manosphere," *New York Times*, June 13, 2017, https://www.nytimes.com/2017/06/13/magazine/hunting-the-manosphere.html.

[20] Drew Harwell, Taylor Lorenz, and Cat Zakrzewski, "Racist Tweets Quickly Surface after Musk Closes Twitter Deal," *Washington Post*, October 28, 2022, https://www.washingtonpost.com/technology/2022/10/28/musk-twitter-racist-posts/.

[21] Ross Douthat, *The Decadent Society: How We Became the Victims of Our Own Success* (New York: Simon and Schuster, 2020).

[22] Shoshana Zuboff, "Big Other: Surveillance Capitalism and the Prospects of an Information Civilization," *Journal of Information Technology* 30, no. 1 (2015): 75–89.

much more. Writing on the social media platform Twitter,[23] Vallor has attributed the general shift of user sentiment from joy to despair to deliberate business plans that disregard the dignity of the person in order to exploit their behaviors and personal information for greed.[24] In her words, "There's no longer anything being promised to us by tech companies that we actually need or asked for. Just more monitoring, more nudging, more draining of our data, our time, our joy." This is only part of the story, however.

We must also consider the disordered state of society, a product of more general trends reshaping contemporary life outside of the Internet. The blogger Tanner Greer argues that social media's problems are not exclusive to the platforms, and are largely caused by a decline in institutional trust due to declining institutional performance, coupled with changing norms around the use and control of certain types of speech.[25] The journalist Willy Staley has chronicled the grossly antisocial behavior found on Twitter through his own firsthand experience, raising alarm over the enormous amount of time users have wasted mired in the seemingly irresistible negativity that directs much of the content found there. In his words, "What's disconcerting is how easy it was to pass all the hours this way. The world just sort of falls away when you're looking at the feed."[26] The feeds of Instagram and TikTok, platforms with an order of magnitude more users than Twitter, are an endless stream of images and videos—many self-indulgent, vulgar, and hurtful to

[23] Twitter is now officially known as "X" following the acquisition of the platform by the billionaire entrepreneur Elon Musk. For the purpose of maintaining continuity in our discussion across different periods of time, we'll continue to refer to it as Twitter throughout the rest of the book.

[24] Shannon Vallor, Twitter, August 16, 2022, 5:53 p.m., https://twitter.com/ShannonVallor/status/1559659655097376768.

[25] Tanner Greer, "The World That Twitter Never Made," The Scholar's Stage, July 15, 2022, https://scholars-stage.org/the-world-that-twitter-never-made/.

[26] Willy Staley, "What Was Twitter, Anyway?," *New York Times*, April 18, 2023, sec. Magazine, https://www.nytimes.com/2023/04/18/magazine/twitter-dying.html.

others. These platforms are intentionally designed to nourish the narcissism of content creators.

Society's embrace of this type of technology indicates the triumph of aggressive secularization and abandonment of virtue in favor of consumerist forces that celebrate the perceived superiority of the self.[27] By living a life without an ultimate purpose, or *telos*, one can find oneself increasingly unmoored. The Internet as it presently exists, therefore, is not a symptom of technology running amok, as many might assume. It is a symptom of a wider social malaise stemming from a separation from God.[28] Writing about salvation on his blog, Father Edmund Waldstein, OCist, identifies the consequences of such an unsettled state of sin, which contribute to the Internet's lack of harmony: "Unable to rest, man is constantly changing his mind and purpose, prying into the affairs of others, seeking to deaden his pain with drugs or alcohol or pseudo-righteous indignation. Miserable himself, he becomes envious of others and maliciously tries to make them miserable in turn."[29] And so social media platforms with a global user base become factories producing misery at an industrial scale on the open market.

This thinking is consonant with messaging emanating from the Vatican on these matters. The three most recent popes have summed up the negative effects of modern society, including modern technology, in one word: alienation.[30] Francis has discussed the alienating effects of technology in multiple encyclicals, letters, and addresses, most notably in his encyclicals *Laudato Si'* and *Fratelli Tutti*.

---

[27] Alasdair MacIntyre, *After Virtue* (London: Bloomsbury, 2013).

[28] Charles Taylor, *The Ethics of Authenticity* (Cambridge, MA: Harvard University Press, 2018).

[29] Edmund Waldstein, "The Eucharist in the Plan of Salvation, First Part," *Sancrucensis* (blog), March 19, 2023, https://sancrucensis.wordpress.com/2023/03/19/the-eucharist-in-the-plan-of-salvation-first-part/.

[30] Pope John Paul II, *Centesimus Annus* 41–42; Pope Benedict XVI, *Caritas in Veritate* 53, 76; Pope Francis, *Evangelii Gaudium* 196; Pope Francis, *Fratelli Tutti* 53.

In *Laudato Si'*, Francis discusses the alienating effects of omnipresent digital technologies, saying that "their influence can stop people from learning how to live wisely, to think deeply, and to love generously" (47). On modern relationship-building, Francis says:

> Real relationships with others, with all the challenges they entail, now tend to be replaced by a type of internet communication which enables us to choose or eliminate relationships at whim, thus giving rise to a new type of contrived emotion which has more to do with devices and displays than with other people and with nature. Today's media do enable us to communicate and to share our knowledge and affections. Yet at times they also shield us from direct contact with the pain, the fears and the joys of others and the complexity of their personal experiences. (47)

In other words, current social technologies are not an adequate substitute for an in-person interaction because they do not provide the same shared depth of experience that comes from such an interaction, where one can see, hear, and feel the emotions of others. Excessive use of current social technologies in place of in-person socializing, when it is feasible, can lead to alienation by depriving the user of these innately human things.

Social technologies also eliminate friction from relationships, allowing people to log off or not respond if interactions become uncomfortable. Vallor argues that the prevalence of these frictionless online interactions prevents people from cultivating the virtue required to maintain meaningful relationships. In her words, "A frictionless world where every social bond and duty was conditional upon the ongoing ability of others to keep us stimulated and pleased would diminish us all."[31] Francis concurs with this in *Fratelli Tutti*, saying: "As silence and careful listening disappear, replaced by a frenzy of texting, this basic structure of sage human

---

[31] Vallor, *Technology and the Virtues*, 164.

communication is at risk. A new lifestyle is emerging, where we create only what we want and exclude all that we cannot control or know instantly and superficially. This process, by its intrinsic logic, blocks the kind of serene reflection that could lead us to a shared wisdom" (49).

Francis and Vallor agree that the superficiality of interaction enabled by social technologies has detrimental effects on society. These frictionless interactions inhibit authentic in-person *dialogue*; current social technologies promote discrete exchange rather than the frank conversation of a good dialogue. On the breakdown of authentic dialogue in online interactions, Francis says in *Fratelli Tutti*:

> Dialogue is often confused with something quite different: the feverish exchange of opinions on social networks, frequently based on media information that is not always reliable. These exchanges are merely parallel monologues. They may attract some attention by their sharp and aggressive tone. But monologues engage no one, and their content is frequently self-serving and contradictory. Indeed, the media's noisy potpourri of facts and opinions is often an obstacle to dialogue, since it lets everyone cling stubbornly to his or her own ideas, interests and choices, with the excuse that everyone else is wrong. It becomes easier to discredit and insult opponents from the outset than to open a respectful dialogue aimed at achieving agreement on a deeper level. (200–201)

In the field of computer science, *human-computer interaction* (HCI) research has found that current social technologies cause people to shy away from conflict online due to such conflicts quickly turning toxic, in spite of the fact that conflict is essential for developing healthy interpersonal relationships. Additionally, even though people shy away from conflict online, they actually desire to discuss challenging topics.[32]

---

[32] Amanda Baughan et al., "Someone Is Wrong on the Internet: Having Hard Conversations in Online Spaces," *Proceedings of the ACM on Human-Computer Interaction* 5, no. CSCW1 (2021): 1–22.

Another key problem with social technologies is the way that their addictive mechanisms cause us to become distracted.[33] In *Technology and the Virtues*, Vallor discusses the addictive nature of social media apps, which cause ethical trouble by hindering the virtue of self-control essential to human well-being.[34] Vallor appeals to John Stuart Mill, who considered the fundamental dilemma underpinning this in an earlier era: "Men lose their high aspirations as they lose their intellectual tastes, because they have not time or opportunity for indulging them; and they addict themselves to inferior pleasures, not because they deliberately prefer them, but because they are either the only pens to which they have access, or the only ones which they are any longer capable of enjoying."[35] Though Mill had no exposure to modern social media technologies, we can see how this statement applies. Not even considering how social media technologies affect our interpersonal communication, we can still see that the addictive mechanisms built into social technologies pull people into cycles where they are constantly checking for notifications and updates, rendering them unable to contemplate higher things.

In *Fratelli Tutti*, Francis describes this phenomenon as such: "Today we can recognize that we fed ourselves on dreams of splendor and grandeur, and ended up consuming distraction, insularity and solitude. We gorged ourselves on networking, and lost the taste of fraternity. We looked for quick and safe results, only to find ourselves overwhelmed by impatience and anxiety. Prisoners of a virtual reality, we lost the taste and flavor of the truly real" (33). Is it possible to escape from this virtual prison of our own making without completely abandoning the technology we use on a daily basis?

---

[33] U.S. Surgeon General, "Social Media and Youth Mental Health," U.S. Department of Health and Human Services, 2023, https://www.hhs.gov/surgeongeneral/priorities/youth-mental-health/social-media/index.html.

[34] Vallor, *Technology and the Virtues*, sec. 7.2.

[35] John Stuart Mill, *Utilitarianism*, 2nd ed. (Cambridge, MA: Hackett, 2001).

A Benedict Option for the Internet?

The many drawbacks of social technologies make it tempting to take a Luddite approach and either rid ourselves of technology entirely or simply view it as a necessary evil and continue using it as is. The Internet is filled to the brim with groups promoting a variety of ideas that are in continuous conflict with one another, making it difficult, if not impossible, for different communities to exist in harmony there. But the technology itself is not necessarily a party to these conflicts, even though it facilitates them. Instead of outright abandoning the technologies we don't like, it is perfectly reasonable to establish alternative spaces centered around human flourishing within the infrastructure of the Internet, but distinct from the centralized platforms that also use the same infrastructure. To do that we will need some philosophical grounding.

Virtue ethics is a philosophical tradition that holds that a moral agent's virtue or character is more fundamental in examining ethical issues than any specific moral rules or principles. Though it's often traced back to the ancient Greek philosophy of Aristotle, virtue ethics encompasses a number of historical and contemporary traditions like Confucianism, Buddhism, and Stoicism under its ethics umbrella. Catholic doctrine for the last seven hundred years has been strongly influenced by virtue ethics through the theological work of St. Thomas Aquinas, who drew heavily from Aristotle. Even before Aquinas, the Catholic intellectual tradition was substantively interacting with virtue ethics, for example, through Augustine's synthesis of Platonic and Neoplatonic thought.

Over the centuries, some virtue ethicists have relied on a comprehensive sketch of human nature based on the notion of the person as a dependent and rational agent to further develop their philosophy. By establishing that each of us must rely on others to thrive, these thinkers argue that virtue isn't exercised in a self-centered way, but instead communally. This in turn leads to the idea of the *common good*, where the positive motivations and character traits of individuals are directed toward the flourishing of groups. In contrast, Vallor, who is a practicing virtue ethicist, prioritizes virtues and character traits as they relate to the individual in order to make recommendations on the development and use of technology. This is compatible with some of the tenets of virtue ethics, but a better path comes into focus when one directs his or her energy beyond the self.

In the twentieth century, virtue ethics experienced a renaissance in part through the writings of the philosopher Alasdair MacIntyre,[36] who claimed that the disappearance of virtue from public and private life coincided with the rise of liberalism and consumer capitalism in modernity, which emphasized individual achievement over flourishing communities. Arguing for a revival of virtue, he pointed to the figure of St. Benedict, the fifth-century monk who established a rule by which one could live a moral life in an age of barbarism following the collapse of Rome, as a prototype for what is needed to overcome the present social crisis. Benedict's *modus operandi* was to establish monasteries joined by the faithful who had withdrawn from society to pursue a spiritual life structured by his rule.

MacIntyre's work in turn inspired the popular yet controversial idea of the *Benedict Option* in Christian circles, whereby orthodox Christians would withdraw from society and form intentional communities in order to preserve their way of life—which some believe has come under withering fire from secular critics proposing that partisan politics, unfettered capitalism, and expressive individualism form a preferable culture.[37] Walling off one's life from society at-large is perhaps a bit extreme for the average person, but there is something to this idea. Leah Libresco, a popular Catholic blogger, has advocated for a more reasonable version of the Benedict Option that on a regular basis brings small groups

---

[36] MacIntyre, *After Virtue*.

[37] Rod Dreher, *The Benedict Option: A Strategy for Christians in a Post-Christian Nation* (New York: Penguin, 2017).

of like-minded Christians together for fellowship and fun by in-corporating prayer into movie nights, book clubs, and any other activity that already has a social dimension.[38] Can something similar be done to restore virtue in virtual spaces?

We suggest that what is needed is a *Benedict Option for the Internet*, which, like St. Benedict's activities in late antiquity, would initially establish small online communities that can thrive under a common framework. If successful, the communities would have the option to grow, eventually turning into something resembling McLuhan's Global Village (much like Christianity grew to become a global village in a different sense). What makes this idea feasible is that the underlying technology (e.g., the computers, network protocols) need not change. New virtual spaces can simply be programmed on top of them: there is nothing stopping the crea-tion of an Internet within the Internet.

And this is already starting to happen, not just within Chris-tianity but across different affinity groups found on the Internet. Smaller groups that are routinely assailed on social media plat-forms with global reach are decamping to alternatives, like Discord and Substack, which limit participation to just group members.[39] Interestingly, there is a historical analog for a social technology that is specific to certain communities: the Bulletin Board System (BBS). In the 1980s and 1990s, amateur computer operators would connect their personal computers to the phone network so that others could dial into them in order to exchange messages and files. Over time, special interest boards were established to support a diverse set of communities spanning everything from homebrew computing to queer interests, and hobby gaming to Christianity. Thus the flight to community-specific infrastructure is very similar to the way things were in the beginning of computer networking

---

[38] Leah Libresco, *Building the Benedict Option: A Guide to Gathering Two or Three Together in His Name* (San Francisco: Ignatius Press, 2018).

[39] Noah Smith, "The New 1970s," *Noahpinion* (blog), July 24, 2023, https://www.noahpinion.blog/p/the-new-1970s.

before the corporate consolidation of the Internet. The media studies scholar Kevin Driscoll believes that a more decentralized Internet where communities more resemble the BBSs of years past is a constructive path forward for improving social technology.[40] But pitfalls exist when using existing software to achieve this goal. In most cases, an intentional design is required to avoid needlessly falling back to the divisions present on the Internet today.

The Design of Virtuous Technology

Virtue ethicists like MacIntyre and Vallor are very helpful in making a compelling case that our lives should be organized around virtue. But they don't provide us with specific guidance on how to do that in all cases. We propose that good software engineering begins with thinking about how a piece of technology will support a community in a healthy way, followed by building the technology according to the principles of virtue that provide that support, and then actively using the technology to do what it was intended for. We need to draw on a specific ethic to formulate virtuous requirements and an implementation regime that is feasible for the programmer, all in order to facilitate a specific user activity. For this, we focus on a sequence of three particular elements as shown in figure 1.1: *Think → Build → Do*.

	Think →	Build →	Do
Enactment	Ethic	Implementation	Activity
Example	Catholic Social Teaching	App	Dialogue

Figure 1.1. A sequence of three essential elements of virtuous technology: *Think → Build → Do*. An example sequence is shown for the form of dialogue Pope Francis advocates for.

---

[40] Kevin Driscoll, *The Modem World: A Prehistory of Social Media* (New Haven, CT: Yale University Press, 2022).

The ethic we will consider in this book is *Catholic Social Teaching*, which is a virtue ethic.[41] Catholic Social Teaching is a virtue-based framework for forming a just world that emphasizes concepts like the significance of motivation and intention in evaluating action, the centrality of the virtues in living well and fulfilling our moral obligations, and the ethical status of both the community and the human person in determining how we evaluate and attempt to shape society.[42] Moreover, in the magisterial document *Inter Mirifica*, Pope Paul VI's primary suggestion for living well with new communications technologies is the cultivation of virtue in both the consumers and producers of content, which can be achieved by applying Catholic Social Teaching.

During the Industrial Revolution, Pope Leo XIII penned *Rerum Novarum*, an encyclical addressing the unjust social structures resulting from industrialization. *Rerum Novarum* is now considered to have prophetic value, and was the first document in the body of thought known today as Catholic Social Teaching. As Catholic Social Teaching has been developed and refined over the course of many encyclicals published since the Industrial Revolution, eight key themes have emerged:[43]

1. Life and Dignity of the Human Person
2. Call to Family, Community, and Participation
3. Rights and Responsibilities

---

[41] Helen Alford, "Virtue Ethics in the Catholic Tradition," in *Handbook of Virtue Ethics in Business and Management*, ed. Alejo José G. Sison, Gregory R. Beabout, and Ignacio Ferrero, International Handbooks in Business Ethics (Dordrecht: Springer Netherlands, 2017), 165–76.

[42] Domènec Melé, "Virtues, Values, and Principles in Catholic Social Teaching," in *Handbook of Virtue Ethics in Business and Management*, 153–64.

[43] United States Conference of Catholic Bishops, "Seven Themes of Catholic Social Teaching," USCCB, 2003, https://www.usccb.org/beliefs-and-teachings /what-we-believe/catholic-social-teaching/seven-themes-of-catholic-social -teaching; Pontifical Council for Justice and Peace, *Compendium of the Social Doctrine of the Church* (Washington, DC: USCCB Publishing, 2005).

4. Option for the Poor and Vulnerable
5. The Dignity of Work and the Rights of Workers
6. Solidarity
7. Subsidiarity
8. Care for God's Creation

Catholic Social Teaching's roots in responding to the Industrial Revolution show that it is not a body of thought that we are adapting to apply to technology, but rather a body of thought created for the specific purpose of responding to the societal changes caused by technology. As such, we find it fitting to apply Catholic Social Teaching to the societal changes caused by today's digital revolution. Note that, like virtue ethics, Catholic Social Teaching doesn't provide specific guidance on how to address social problems. Instead, it is meant to be high-level doctrine that provokes discernment and discussion. Thus we strive to develop specific guidance for its application to digital technology in this book. We hope Catholic Social Teaching will prove to have as much prophetic value when applied to the Digital Age as it did to the Industrial Revolution.

Moving to the implementation of software, we argue that programmers should rely on emerging practices from HCI that emphasize the dignity of the user. HCI is a human-centered approach to computing, stressing novel design choices that enhance the experience of a person using a computer. There are many different ways to go about creating such enhancements, largely centered around specific user requirements that intersect with personal and group preferences. There is quite a bit of flexibility with respect to what these can be, and some are compatible with the themes of Catholic Social Teaching.

As a notable example of this, in their article "Reclaiming Attention: Christianity and HCI," the computer scientists Alexis Hiniker and Jacob Wobbrock explore how technology design can support Christian users in living out their faith. The authors highlight three ways in which Christianity calls its followers to live in relationship: relationship with God, relationship with others, and relationship with creation. They point to the *attention economy* as a reason for why current social technologies hinder relationship building and call for a shift from designing for engagement to designing for the radical prioritization of relationships. To achieve this relationship-based design agenda, they propose designing user interfaces that enable users to attune themselves to God, others, and creation. They also propose designing technologies that foster secure attachments through emotional responsiveness and availability. The authors conclude that "the attention economy and the work of relationship building share the same currency and compete for the same scarce resource of human attention. As long as HCI designers have other plans for users' attention, those users will be compromised in their ability to invest in relationships."[44]

In this book, we are primarily concerned with social technologies. That means any technology where the activity of users centers around communication. Here we advocate for a particular mode of communication: dialogue. As stated in a dialogue training manual developed at the University of Notre Dame for discussion-based courses, "In everyday life, a dialogue is any conversation in which all participants share perspectives on a question or idea and listen carefully enough to empathize with each other and develop their views."[45] In a dialogue, the Socratic method is frequently employed to promote critical thinking and understand the underlying assumptions of the participants. Engaging in dialogue effectively allows all participants to grow in virtue as they actively listen to others and respond in a thoughtful way.

---

[44] Alexis Hiniker and Jacob O. Wobbrock, "Reclaiming Attention: Christianity and HCI," *Interactions* 29, no. 4 (2022): 40–44.
[45] Paul Blaschko et al., "Training Manual," Sheedy Family Program in Economy, Enterprise, and Society Dialogue, University of Notre Dame, July 2022, https://ethicsatwork.nd.edu/resources/dialogue-training-manual.

What we propose through this activity is not a utopian Silicon Valley project destined to reduce discourse to bland corporate language or hollow groupthink through the control of speech. As noted above, a healthy amount of friction, which subtly suggests that ideas can be reconsidered without alienating anyone, should be present in a good dialogue. This is a natural consequence of the presence of a diversity of ideas. But instead of driving a wedge between participants, dialogue should bring them closer together as they work through problems in a way that is not possible when a lone person is thinking in isolation. As McLuhan emphasizes, "When information is brushed against information . . . the results are startling and effective."[46]

A Path Forward for Anyone Interested in Technology

In the rest of this book we present a guide for anyone concerned with both the use and development of social technologies. We discuss how the Catholic Church has left somewhat incomplete its teachings on technology ethics thus far—particularly the integration of ethical principles in the design of software. We then propose Catholic Social Teaching as a framework for evaluating and designing social technologies, thus filling that gap (figure 1.2). The framework is meant to be accessible to both technical and nontechnical people, and useful to both devout Christians and secular parties with a vested interest in virtue ethics and technology. In line with this, we draw from a variety of sources, some faith-based and some not, to build a case on a set of intriguing ideas that have stood the test of time and will appeal to a broad audience. Parishes can make good use of this volume for instructional purposes, especially for young adult ministries.

[46] Marshall McLuhan and Quentin Fiore, *The Medium Is the Massage: An Inventory of Effects* (Richmond, CA: Gingko Press, 2001).

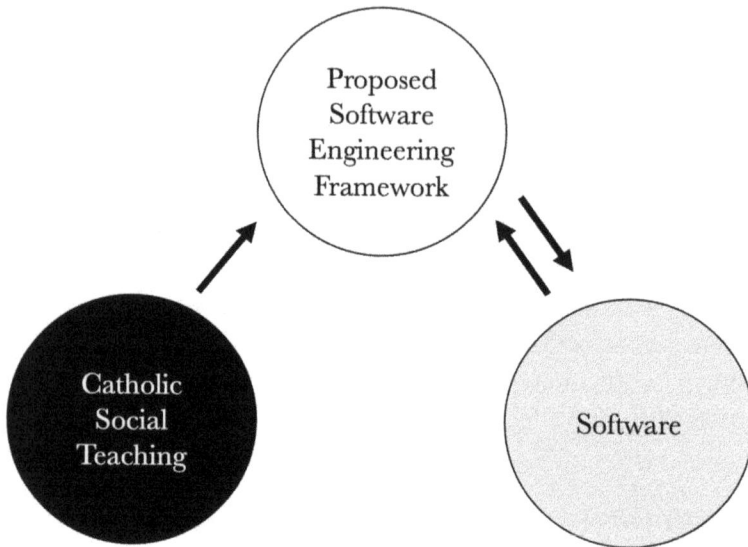

Figure 1.2. Our proposed software engineering framework sits between Catholic Social Teaching, which imparts its principles upon it, and the software itself, which influences and is influenced by the framework.

The rest of this book is organized as follows. In chapter 2 we more fully introduce Catholic Social Teaching and connect it to technology in the twenty-first century. In chapter 3 we discuss the ins and outs of dialogue, and how it applies to social technologies. Chapter 4 moves to the design of technology, and discusses how Catholic Social Teaching can be translated to *design principles* for software. In chapter 5, we examine several case studies drawn from current social media and examine them through the lens of our Catholic Social Teaching–based framework. As we will see, the Internet can be a space for evangelization and communion, but it leaves much to be desired in its current form. Finally, to conclude the book in chapter 6, we take a brief look at how our framework can apply to radically new technologies like *generative artificial intelligence*. Throughout this book, we make the case for a new

techno-optimism rooted in the Catholic tradition. This hopefulness in the potential good of digital technology has not been expressed beyond the Church's writing. We propose that by using
Catholic Social Teaching as a framework, we can express this
hopefulness by doing what is necessary to bring that good into
being.

Chapter
TWO

Historical Background
of Catholic Social Teaching

We believe the Catholic Church can, and should, be a guiding voice in directing technology to be built for good. The church has the mission of being a prophetic voice on issues of human dignity and social justice both to Catholics and to the whole world.[1] This may seem surprising, given public hostility toward some church teachings in today's culture—particularly in America. However, the church's social teaching has in fact had a tangible impact on public policy. For example, the US military teaches its troops Just War Theory, which comes from the Catholic moral tradition.[2] More recently, Pope Francis released a handbook on the ethics of artificial intelligence as a response to multiple Silicon Valley businesses looking to the Vatican for guidance.[3] Through our own engagement with the Catholic intellectual tradition, we have come

---

[1] Pope Francis, *Humanam Progressionem*, August 17, 2016, https://www.vatican.va/content/francesco/en/motu_proprio/documents/papa-francesco-motu-proprio_20160817_humanam-progressionem.html.

[2] J. Toby Reiner, "New Directions in Just-War Theory," *Monographs, Books, and Publications* 397 (July 30, 2018), https://press.armywarcollege.edu/monographs/397.

[3] Mehul Reuben Das, "PopeGPT: Pope Francis Releases 'The Vatican Handbook to Develop Ethical AI,'" Firstpost, July 3, 2023, https://www.firstpost.com

to believe that Catholic Social Teaching in particular is an apt framework for guiding the development of the social technologies that are at the forefront of society's engagement with technology. In this chapter, we will explain the history and development of Catholic Social Teaching, as well as justify its relevance to technology, in order to share our insights with those who may be less versed in the social tradition of the Catholic Church.

Catholic Social Teaching is the body of work in Catholic thought that addresses issues of the respect for the human person that support "the rights which flow from his dignity as a creature."[4] Catholic Social Teaching articulates how to build a just society that emphasizes the *common good*: "the sum total of social conditions which allow people, either as groups or as individuals, to reach their fulfillment more fully and more easily" (*Gaudium et Spes* 26). In this society, economic systems are set up such that everyone is able to participate in the economy and earn enough money to support their families and live a dignified life with access to all the resources they need to thrive. These economic systems also cross state borders, with wealthy countries aiding poorer countries, and countries cooperating to prevent war in order to keep all lines of human development open. People who have more than what they need will share what they have with the poor and reject a lifestyle of superabundance. This society is not just one where each person thrives on an individual level but one in which human flourishing is dependent on the strengthening of our communal ties.

Catholic Social Teaching acknowledges that even though the formation of a perfectly just society is impossible in this life, working toward building such a society (to the extent that we are able) can bear much fruit in our communities. We should do so because

---

/tech/news-analysis/pope-francis-releases-the-vatican-handbook-to-develop -ethical-ai-12817132.html.

[4] *Catechism of the Catholic Church*, 2nd ed. (United States Catholic Conference —Libreria Editrice Vaticana, 1997), 1930.

our faith calls us to perform good works as Christ did in the gospels. Moreover, Catholic Social Teaching is a virtue ethic because it is concerned with who we become as we work toward building a more just world.

The Development of Catholic Social Teaching

As we mentioned in chapter 1, the earliest document in the body of work considered as Catholic Social Teaching is *Rerum Novarum*, written in 1891. As the Industrial Revolution began, the economies in Europe and the United States moved from systems of small-scale farming and sales of artisan handcrafted goods to factory-based manufacturing. This new system of factory work led to stark economic inequality and injustices against the dignity of the workers, including lower-than-living wages and harsh working conditions. As a response, Pope Leo XIII penned *Rerum Novarum*, an encyclical addressing the unjust social structures resulting from industrialization. Thus Catholic Social Teaching began in response to societal changes caused by engineering. *Rerum Novarum* opened the door for the institutional church to comment on the social order as it is shaped by technological innovation.

From *Rerum Novarum* to the present day, any church teaching concerned with human dignity and the common good in society is considered to be a part of Catholic Social Teaching. This body of thought developed over the course of the twentieth and twenty-first centuries through the release of encyclicals, pastoral letters, and other papal and episcopal documents commenting on contemporary social issues in light of the Gospel. These issues include economic justice related to the just distribution of goods and wealth, nuclear disarmament and promotion of nonviolent strategies to achieve world peace, migration, global development, criticism of the death penalty, condemnation of racism, emphasis of the dignity of women, the interplay of evangelization and justice, and care for the natural environment. To frame our thinking around these issues and to guide our response to them, a number of common themes have emerged. These themes include the eight themes highlighted in chapter 1: Life and Dignity of the Human Person; Call to Family, Community, and Participation; Rights and Responsibilities; Option for the Poor and Vulnerable; the Dignity of Work and Rights of Workers; Solidarity; Subsidiarity; and Care for God's Creation. We will discuss each of these themes in more depth in chapter 4, especially how they can direct our response to social technologies.

Catholic Social Teaching's invitation to dialogue about how to enact justice in the world is extended beyond the Catholic faithful. Many documents of Catholic Social Teaching are addressed to "all people of goodwill." Through Catholic Social Teaching, the Catholic Church reaches out to all members of the human family who desire to work for justice and invites them to bring their unique backgrounds into conversation to work together to build a more just world.

Catholic Social Teaching as It Relates to Technology

Why should we consider Catholic Social Teaching when building technology today? One link lies in its origin. As mentioned earlier, the first document of Catholic Social Teaching, *Rerum Novarum*, was written as a response to the societal changes caused by the Industrial Revolution. Many of the social ills addressed in Catholic Social Teaching arose alongside technological developments, and as a result, many Catholic Social Teaching documents comment explicitly on the role of technology.

Catholic Social Teaching also teaches us how to live well in community. It underscores that we are a global family, and that alone we cannot flourish or be saved.[5] Because Catholic Social Teaching is so focused on interpersonal ties, it is incredibly relevant to social

[5] Pope Francis, *Fratelli Tutti* 32, 137; Pope Francis, *Evangelii Gaudium* 113; *Catechism of the Catholic Church* 1905.

technologies in particular. First, social technologies have trans-
formed the way we connect with one another and stay in relationship and community in the modern world. Second, some social
technologies, especially social media, have been designed in ways
that are addictive, promote comparison with others, and encourage
consumerism. Catholic Social Teaching is concerned with how the
built environment affects our ability to become virtuous people,[6]
and the design of social technologies is certainly affecting that. The
technologies of tomorrow will build on the technologies of today,
so the extent to which our descendants will be able to grow in the
authentic community that is so vital to our human experience and
necessary for our salvation hinges on how technologies are built
in the present moment.

Many of the themes of Catholic Social Teaching, even when not
originally mentioned in the context of technological progress, can
shed light on how to evaluate contemporary technology. One example of this is Catholic Social Teaching's criticism of profit as a
primary economic motive (*Populorum Progressio* 26). While profit
is important to an extent for a business to survive and in order to
pay workers a just wage, Catholic Social Teaching warns of the
dangers of maximizing profit at the expense of the dignity of the
company's workers *and* customers. Social media companies today
tend to pursue profit at the expense of the dignity of their users
by following an attention economy business model.[7] In exploiting
an attention economy model, social media companies design their
applications in an addictive way that captures the user's attention
for the purpose of showing them more advertising, thereby making
more money.

In addition to having a number of teachings that can be applied
to the evaluation of technology, Catholic Social Teaching also
contains a body of writing that comments specifically on the place
of technology in society. All three of us authors have noticed two

---

[6] Pope Paul VI, *Populorum Progressio* 17; Pope Francis, *Laudato Si'* 159.
[7] Hiniker and Wobbrock, "Reclaiming Attention," 40–44.

camps of technology users among our friends. Some people we know idolize technology and push for a techno-utopia: "Technology will solve all our problems!" Others, seeing the harms caused by modern technologies, attempt to adopt a neo-Luddite attitude toward it: "It's a sin to use a smartphone!" Catholic Social Teaching, however, espouses neither a techno-utopian nor a neo-Luddite attitude. Rather, it promotes the development of technologies that serve humanity in an authentic way.

The following examples from Catholic Social Teaching illustrate this view that technology itself is subservient to human direction. In his 2009 encyclical *Caritas in Veritate,* Pope Benedict XVI notes that neither "idealizing technical progress" nor "contemplating the utopia of a return to humanity's original natural state" is the right way to go (14). In his 1981 encyclical *Laborem Exercens,* Pope John Paul II states there is a human vocation to co-create with God through work (25). By extension, when a person engages in the work of building technology, they are potentially engaging in the noble pursuit of co-creating with God. Lest a Luddite think that technology isn't a noble creation, Pope John XXIII said in his 1963 encyclical *Pacem in Terris* that "the progress of science and the inventions of technology show above all the infinite greatness of God" (3). Benedict XVI even argues that fighting for a world with no development or progress (including technological developments and progress) indicates a lack of trust in both man and God (*Caritas in Veritate* 14). Given the current landscape of technologies, it may be hard to believe that creating technology is a reflection of our likeness to God. Catholic Social Teaching tells us that if technology is created well it can actually help us grow in our relationship with God and grow in the fullest understanding of our humanity.

Adopting a Luddite approach toward all technology would be to reject the good fruits of those who developed the technologies as an expression of their creation in the image and likeness of God. At the same time, technology contributes to and advances many social problems criticized in Catholic Social Teaching—if there had been no industrialization, there would have been no reason to critique its effects in *Rerum Novarum*. Catholic Social Teaching is quick to reject the bad effects of technology and any mindset that makes an idol out of it, while reminding us of the powerfully good potential it has. John XXIII acknowledges that while technology can make great contributions to civilization, it is not the highest good (*Mater et Magistra* 175). He also notes that while we may think we can use technology to achieve the highest state of development apart from God, we are routinely confronted with cases that indicate limits to technological intervention (209). As an example, today an increasing amount of technology is being deployed at schools with the hope that it will improve educational outcomes. However, research shows that only a moderate amount of technological intervention has a beneficial effect on education.[8]

It is impossible to make a blanket statement that all technology is inherently good or inherently evil. Rather, the technology that we build mirrors our existing values. This is why Catholic Social Teaching simultaneously paints an optimistic view of technology and strongly criticizes it: the societal values built into a particular technology influence its potential for goodness. Benedict XVI notes that "in technology, seen as the product of his genius, man recognizes himself and forges his own humanity . . . for this reason, technology is never merely technology. It reveals man and his aspirations towards development" (*Caritas in Veritate* 69). Francis says something similar in his 2015 encyclical *Laudato Si'*: "We have to accept that technological products are not neutral, for they create a framework which ends up conditioning lifestyles and shaping social possibilities along the lines dictated by the

---

[8] Ben Kesling, "Technology in Classrooms Doesn't Always Boost Education Results, OECD Says," *Wall Street Journal*, September 15, 2015, https://www.wsj.com/articles/technology-in-classrooms-doesnt-always-boost-education-results-oecd-says-1442343420; AI Research Group for the Centre for Digital Culture, *Encountering Artificial Intelligence: Ethical and Anthropological Investigations*, ed. Matthew J. Gaudet et al. (Portland, OR: Pickwick Press, 2024), 170–79.

interests of certain powerful groups. Decisions which may seem purely instrumental are in reality decisions about the kind of society we want to build" (107).

Benedict XVI emphasizes the way our humanity permeates technology: "Even when we work through satellites or through remote electronic impulses, our actions always remain human" (*Caritas in Veritate* 70). These ideas from Benedict XVI and Francis tell us that because our humanity permeates the technology we build, the ills of technology today are actually reflections of humanity's fallen state. The good news is that as humanity has been redeemed by Jesus Christ, our technology is also able to be redeemed.[9] We have a choice to build our technology with virtuous Christian values in mind.

But technology is not a panacea.[10] In *Laudato Si'*, Francis is critical of the *technocratic paradigm*, a mindset that views everything as a problem to be solved with science and technology (101–12). Francis says that while we don't have to get rid of technology, we should consider how it is serving us and solving our concrete problems (112) rather than get caught up in accepting "every advance in technology with a view to profit, without concern for its potentially negative impact on human beings" (109) or in "unrestrained delusions of grandeur" (114) where we try to make the most impressive technologies possible for no real purpose other than the idolization of that technology. This mindset is seemingly exemplified in Meta CEO Mark Zuckerberg, whose enthusiastic and wholehearted embrace of both metaverse technologies and artificial intelligence[11] leaves one wondering if he is

---

[9] Bo Bonner and Brett Robinson, "Fall Conference 2022—Digital Temples of the Holy Ghost," de Nicola Center for Ethics and Culture, 2022, https://www.youtube.com/watch?v=CdeWXBGrByI.

[10] Pope John Paul II, *Sollicitudo Rei Socialis* 41.

[11] Naomi Nix, "Facebook Pivoted to the Metaverse. Now It Wants to Show off Its AI," *Washington Post*, May 14, 2023, https://www.washingtonpost.com/technology/2023/05/14/meta-generative-ai-metaverse/.

really thinking through the potential impact of these technologies on humanity or just embracing them for their novelty.

Applying Catholic Social Teaching to Build and Use Technology Well

So how should we use technology? We should reject techno-utopianism that prioritizes novel technological innovation over human dignity and the common good. Catholic Social Teaching tells us that "economics and technology have no meaning except from man whom they should serve" (*Populorum Progressio* 34). On the other hand, this also means technology can be given a positive meaning when used for the service of the common good. Even when Francis criticizes the technocratic paradigm in *Laudato Si'*, he makes sure to highlight that when technology is directed well, it can provide us many means of improving our quality of life, including through the provision of important public utilities and new opportunities to encounter beauty (103).

Catholic Social Teaching from the 1960s points out that technology is a necessity for human progress (*Populorum Progressio* 25) and says specifically that "it is indeed clear that the Church has always taught and continues to teach that advances in science and technology and the prosperity resulting therefrom are truly to be counted as good things and regarded as signs of the progress of civilization" (*Mater et Magistra* 246). Catholic Social Teaching also highlights that technology can positively impact human development when it improves the standard of living for all[12] and can assist the worker (*Laborem Exercens* 5). It also confirms the value of man's use of technology to subdue the earth and obtain life's necessities (*Mater et Magistra* 189).

---

[12] Joseph Gremillion, "Medellin Documents," in *The Gospel of Peace and Justice: Catholic Social Teaching Since Pope John* (Maryknoll, NY: Orbis Books, 1976), 451.

How do we build technology in a way that enables it to serve humanity rather than promote a false techno-utopia? Catholic Social Teaching suggests a general attitude to adopt in this regard. The attitude is one that considers human values (*Pacem in Terris* 149), acknowledges that technology isn't the solution to every problem (*Sollicitudo Rei Socialis* 41), and prioritizes deepening social relationships over technical advances (*Gaudium et Spes* 35). These ideas also exist in the secular realm. In his book *Geek Heresy*, computer scientist Kentaro Toyama argues that, when trying to solve problems related to poverty and global development, investing in people is more important than investing in technology, and that technology merely serves as an amplifier for the good work done by people.[13] Although technology can assist us in solving human problems, we must be thoughtful in both the design and employment of technology. Benedict XVI and Francis both note that making technological decisions with moral responsibility is the key to forming a world where we are free from technological paradigms (*Laudato Si'* 105; *Caritas in Veritate* 70). In chapter 4, we'll discuss how the main themes of Catholic Social Teaching can serve as the "human values" underpinning technology design to guide it toward human flourishing.

Catholic Social Teaching as It Relates to Social Technologies

In this book, we have chosen to focus on social technologies because communication is at the heart of the communal human experience. In addition to commenting on technology in a general sense, from the 1960s through the present day, Catholic Social Teaching has continually called the faithful to reflect specifically on the influence of technologies that allow people to communicate (*Pacem in Terris* 90; *Caritas in Veritate* 14). For example, mass media has been singled out as a technology that can increase our

---

[13] Kentaro Toyama, *Geek Heresy* (New York: PublicAffairs, 2015).

ability to evangelize,[14] unite the isolated,[15] foster solidarity,[16] and build connections that actively help to promote justice in the world.[17]

We do in fact see these good fruits from today's technologies. In terms of evangelization, we know multiple people for whom Catholic content on YouTube and Twitter played a major part in their decisions to become Catholic.[18] Zoom gatherings helped us socialize during the COVID-19 lockdowns, uniting the isolated. Finally, social media platforms have fostered a number of conversations about social justice that we didn't have at the same scale previously; one of many such examples is the discussion that emerged on social media after the tragic murder of George Floyd in 2020.

Of course, not all of the changes brought by new social technologies are positive. As early as the 1960s, Catholic Social Teaching criticized how new mass media allowed people to form and maintain more social ties without fostering a depth of relationship (*Gaudium et Spes* 6). This problem continues with today's social media platforms, where it's easy to have hundreds or even thousands of connections on Facebook, Instagram, or Twitter, see their updates regularly, and know what's going on in their lives, but never actually have a conversation with them. Because of this, as we mentioned in chapter 1, Francis has commented extensively on the effect social media has on society. This includes the way it undermines the depth of our thought and the generosity of our

[14] Pope Paul VI, *Evangelii Nuntiandi* 45; Pope John Paul II, "36th World Communications Day."

[15] Pope Benedict XVI, "47th World Communications Day."

[16] Pope Francis, "Video Message to the TED Conference in Vancouver," 7; Pope Francis, "Message for the 2014 World Communications Day," 113.

[17] Gremillion, "Medellin Documents," 454.

[18] Louisa was the baptism and confirmation sponsor for a young man whom she had previously never met but was connected to through a mutual friend in his RCIA class. The reason he couldn't find a sponsor was that he had come to Catholicism through videos featuring Fr. Mike Schmitz on YouTube, and he didn't actually know many Catholics in real life!

love, enabling us to "eliminate relationships at whim" and shielding us from the inherent and good "complexity of . . . personal experiences" (*Laudato Si'* 47).

The most recent papal encyclical as of the writing of this book, *Fratelli Tutti*, discusses extensively the effect of modern technology on social relationships. It is an encyclical on human brotherhood and, having been published during the isolation of the COVID-19 pandemic, would be remiss if it didn't discuss the impact of social media on human relationships. Francis argues that today's digital technologies provide an illusion of communication rather than authentic communication. This illusion of communication may cause us to think we're building relationships, but Francis argues that by not being authentic, it actually "disguise[s] and expand[s] . . . individualism" (43). He also argues that the frenzied communication encouraged by texting discourages careful listening and thoughtful reflection. The flood of information we have access to online doesn't promote genuine wisdom that comes from a mature encounter with the truth (47–50).

Francis proposes an antidote to the societal ills caused by social media: a practice of authentic dialogue (*Fratelli Tutti* 198). While social media can shield us from having to engage with others on a deep level, "true, honest dialogue commits us to love of God, neighbor and self, and helps us to deepen the experience of encounter with others."[19] Unlike today's social media platforms, which often don't allow for a mature encounter with the truth, an authentic dialogue is ordered toward the truth. Through dialogue, participants come to a greater understanding of the truth both by critically examining their own beliefs and by lovingly engaging with people who hold beliefs contrary to theirs. Strong relationships are at the heart of good dialogue, so our current social technologies may fail

---

[19] United States Conference of Catholic Bishops, "Loving Our Neighbor through Dialogue," 2021, USCCB, https://www.usccb.org/resources/Loving-our-Neighbor-through-Dialogue.pdf.

to help us foster good dialogue if they also fail to help us cultivate deep relationships.

Building Better Social Technologies in Light of Catholic Social Teaching

As we have seen, Catholic Social Teaching has criticized social technologies for inhibiting us from thinking wisely and deeply and from loving generously and forming strong relationships. At the same time, Catholic Social Teaching expresses that technology, including social technologies, can be powerfully good, but only if human values are considered when building the technology. Technology built in this way would enable social relationships to go deeper, bringing us into greater communion with our human family. Combining this guidance with Francis's call to love our neighbor through dialogue, we propose that dialogue is one key human factor to consider when developing any social technology. Although it is not the only human factor to consider, we find dialogue to be so important that we will dedicate the next chapter to discussing its significance and how it can be enacted well in both in-person and online spaces.

Chapter THREE

Dialogue and Social Technologies

As engineers and computer scientists with an interest in technology ethics, we're always having conversations with colleagues and friends about the role technology plays in our lives. Inevitably, the conversation turns to social media and how algorithms shape our interactions. Frequently, these conversations lead our interlocutors to say, "I guess I should just throw out my cell phone" or "Maybe I need to delete all my social media." We, the authors, have felt this too. Is there anything worth preserving from this technology? Should everyone go back to flip phones, which don't support the use of interactive social media platforms?

A couple of years ago, one of us (Megan) tried this. She put her smartphone aside for Lent and replaced it with something called the Light Phone.[1] The Light Phone is intentionally designed to be a minimal smartphone, created to encourage the user to look away from the screen and into the world around them. The interface is simple: the phone only supports calling, texting, audio playback, and a primitive calculator. And the screen itself is a dim grayscale LCD that has a slow refresh rate, making the phone rather cumbersome to use. Megan's report on her experience with the phone follows:

---

[1] "The Light Phone," accessed July 6, 2023, https://www.thelightphone.com/.

A few hours in, I hated it and was itching to scroll through Instagram again. Later that day, I was meeting friends for dinner at a new restaurant and had to take screenshots of maps on my iPad so I wouldn't get lost—I was terrified of making the wrong turn. While the Light Phone does support maps, I could never get them to work properly. About a week in, while teaching my technology ethics class, my students asked how the experience was going. I was really scared to admit how hard of a time I was having. I ultimately shared with the students that I really missed my iPhone. This led to a discussion about the power social technologies have over our lives. I did persist through Lent, frequently feeling like an addict who was going through withdrawal. I ended up needing to go back to my smartphone by the end of the trial because I was having a flare-up of a chronic injury and couldn't use my right arm. So, it was necessary to use the talk-to-text feature of my iPhone.

Megan's experience with the Light Phone revealed a few general truths about social technologies like smartphones:

- Networked devices provide users with a superhighway of information that makes it convenient to look up anything quickly.

- Not having digital maps made nearly every car trip harder.

- Travel apps, not allowed on Light Phones, make the process of traveling so much easier, including the ability to rebook flights, receive gate updates at the airport, and hail ride-shares.

- Streaming makes it possible to listen to any song or podcast whenever the user wants. The Light Phone requires pre-downloading of that content via Wi-Fi. But if one ignores the convenience factor of downloading on the go, audio-based technology can be good in either case because it doesn't force the user to stare at a screen.

- The accessibility features of mobile devices serve an important role, helping to support day-to-day activity when one has limited mobility.

- Connecting with friends and family is limited when not video chatting or connecting through social media apps.

So while it is easy to want to throw out all modern technology, there are valid and even good reasons to continue using our smartphones.

We see from this example that social technologies enhance our lives in a myriad of ways. However, today's social media ends up having detrimental effects due to it being increasingly designed to conform to the attention economy.[2] Most of the social technologies we use today have come from Silicon Valley and follow the values of those living there in the 1990s and early 2000s.[3] Silicon Valley has given us a limited number of options for how social technologies should be built. Instead of what we commonly see today, could an economic model other than advertising back the apps? And how might that inform the design of the platforms? Regrettably, we appear locked into the existing regime because of the financial success of the attention economy, which couples advertising with continuous user engagement. The attention economy's impact on social media has made it harder to practice virtue[4] and has established many of our social connections through algorithmic means.[5] More recently, new apps like BeReal[6] have proposed an alternative strategy. This second generation of social media is designed around the notion of authenticity, prompting

[2] "The Attention Economy," Center for Humane Technology, accessed August 3, 2023, https://www.humanetech.com/youth/the-attention-economy.

[3] Rob Reich, Mehran Sahami, and Jeremy M. Weinstein, *System Error: Where Big Tech Went Wrong and How We Can Reboot* (New York: HarperCollins, 2021), chap. 2; Sheila Jasanoff, *The Ethics of Invention: Technology and the Human Future*, 1st ed., Norton Global Ethics Series (New York: W.W. Norton, 2016), chap. 6.

[4] Sigal Samuel, "It's Hard to Be a Moral Person. Technology Is Making It Harder," Vox, July 27, 2021, https://www.vox.com/the-highlight/22585287/technology-smartphones-gmail-attention-morality.

[5] *The Social Dilemma*, Netflix, accessed August 3, 2023, https://www.netflix.com/watch/81254224?source=35.

[6] "BeReal. Your Friends for Real," BeReal, accessed August 3, 2023, https://bereal.com/en/press/.

users to capture candid photos with minimal staging and subsequent editing. While still experimental, these apps are drawing venture funding—but have not proved to be viable businesses yet.[7]

Catholic Social Teaching can serve as a third way forward for technology design to encourage better social habits and foster virtue among users. There are several key themes of Catholic Social Teaching that we will dig into in the next chapter, but for now, we want to highlight a way to enact Catholic Social Teaching in day-to-day interactions. Dialogue is a practice that can be used to raise, engage, and live out the themes of Catholic Social Teaching.[8]

In the first chapter of this book we introduced a sequence for designing technologies: Think → Build → Do. As we approach technology through the sequence, it enables activities (Do) that happen through an interface (Build) that is created based on a particular philosophy or set of principles (Think). As we consider the activities and philosophies built into a technology, we need to avoid the lure of the advertiser-driven attention economy. There exists a different approach, one that is centered on the human person and encourages them to engage with philosophical principles derived from virtue ethics, which drive the build of the technology itself. To do this, we introduce dialogue as the activity enabled by a social technology to put Catholic Social Teaching, especially the eight main themes we highlight in this book, into practice.

Dialogue is what happens when two or more people engage with an idea together: they build off of each other's thoughts and experiences to more deeply uncover the truth.[9] When sharing

---

[7] Krystal Scanlon, "BeReal Still Has Potential for Advertisers, but Its Hype Period Is Well and Truly Over," Digiday, February 28, 2023, https://digiday.com /marketing/bereal-still-has-potential-for-advertisers-but-its-hype-period-is-well -and-truly-over/.

[8] United States Conference of Catholic Bishops, "Civilize It: Loving Our Neighbor through Dialogue | Amar a Nuestro Vecino a Través Del Diálogo," USCCB, accessed August 4, 2023, https://www.usccb.org/resources/civilize-it-loving -our-neighbor-through-dialogue-amar-nuestro-vecino-traves-del-dialogo.

[9] Blaschko et al., "Training Manual."

stories about our lives, we are frequently more willing to learn from one another. The interactions we have on the Internet can benefit from this form of dialogue, so that we can experience each other's humanity in a constructive way instead of angrily escalating or abruptly retreating in the face of divisive rhetoric. Through an encounter with the uniqueness of other people, we develop in new ways. On social media, communication frequently takes on a click-bait form, where each argument is presented as its logical extreme to catch our attention and provide nothing more. As designers of technology ourselves, we have no interest in clickbait, and you shouldn't either.

This great capacity for the sharing of information on the Internet is something good for humanity: we can learn efficiently and can grow closer to the truth. Users look to platforms like Twitter and YouTube as places for hearing the latest news and learning new things. Many students today will view educational videos online if they are confused about a topic in a textbook. We learn best together. The ancients knew this and used dialogue as a tool for teaching and engaging with philosophy. Given the power of dialogue, we introduce it here as a key to building human-centered social technologies.

Why Dialogue?

Here is a thought experiment: Think back to the last time you had a really great conversation—one where everyone was engaged and interested. What features did that conversation have? How did the participants interact with one another? Where did you gather? In person? On a video call? Chatting via text online? Did everyone present similar ideas? Or did they present contrasting views? Were they agreeable? Argumentative? Did everyone involved have the same background?

Dialogue is important because people learn better together. As you're reading this now, there is a form of one-directional dialogue that is happening from us, the authors, to you, the reader. But how much better (and perhaps more efficient) would it be if you could ask us questions as you read this chapter? In line with this, Pope Francis reminds us that "we need to communicate with each other, to discover the gifts of each person, to promote that which unites us, and to regard our differences as an opportunity to grow in mutual respect. Patience and trust are called for in such dialogue, permitting individuals, families and communities to hand on the values of their own culture and welcome the good that comes from others' experiences" (*Fratelli Tutti* 134). We, the authors of this book, would become better teachers if we could respond to your questions. And you might ask a question that gets us to think deeper about one of the ideas that we are sharing with you. That's an example of good dialogue. By communicating back and forth, we both learn better and help one another uncover the truth of the matter at hand.

Rather than asking what the right answer is, dialogue begins with questions about how some shared truth might appear differently to different people from their unique vantage points. With dialogue, we ask "how?" and "why?" questions rather than ones that can be answered with a simple "yes" or "no."[10] This deep questioning is a method that encourages an encounter between persons and can be a method to uncover the common good, one that supports our individuality and community.

When teaching students about dialogue, we begin with a picture of a sculpture of an elephant. That image is used to show the students that from different angles, the elephant looks completely different. From the front and back sides we might see entirely different things (e.g., the ears, a tail). Does this mean that we are looking at two different objects? Of course not. Does it also mean that the sculpture doesn't have objective features? Also no. This is one of the remarkable things about dialogue: we approach truth from our own unique perspectives. That truth may reveal itself initially as something unique to each person, but as we converse

---

[10] Blaschko et al.

with one another, we begin to identify similarities and get closer to defining the truth.

Asking Strong Questions

Strong questions are the foundation for thoughtful dialogue.[11] One needs to ask them to grapple with the big questions of life. How do we do this? Strong questions usually begin with a "how?" or "why?" in order to ask something that can't be answered in one word. Formulating a strong question requires thoughtful reflection over a period of time before jumping into dialogue with others. After you've come up with a few questions of your own, consult figure 3.1 for some tips for actually asking them in dialogue.

Tips for Strong Dialogue
• Begin with what you know, a topic or idea that is personally interesting to you. Usually, if you are interested in topic you have thought about it for some time and know the context around it. This adds depth to the dialogue.
• Ask out of genuine curiosity. This helps build intellectual virtue, by admitting what you do not know.
• Ask one question at a time. This helps you to dive deep into one area rather than treading water near the surface, trying to go several directions at once but never making progress.
• Be comfortable with silence. Giving others space to respond can sometimes feel like it is ruining the cadence of the conversation, but silence provides space for reflection.
• Resist self-deprecation. Rather than saying: "This might be a dumb question but . . ." just ask the question. Curiosity and confidence will serve the dialogue much better.

Figure 3.1. Tips for asking strong "how" and "why" questions in dialogue.

[11] Blaschko et al.

Key Dispositions of Good Dialogue

The process of dialogue then requires several things from those entering into it together (figure 3.2). The following four principles are adapted from a dialogue training manual created at Notre Dame:[12] (1) Participants need enough space to be able to reflect on what is being said. This is called *thoughtful reflection*. (2) Dialogue participants need to be heard; to do this they need to enter the conversation with *vulnerability*. (3) Each member of the dialogue (and there can be many) needs a sense of *co-ownership*. (4) A good partner in conversation maintains a posture of *openness* to all members, even in online conversations where it's easier to be distracted. To learn from others, dialogue participants need to be willing to listen to one another. An earnest dialogue partner will create the right sort of conversational tension that leads to growth instead of counterproductive argumentation. Let's discuss each of these tenets of dialogue in more detail to gain a better understanding of what is required.

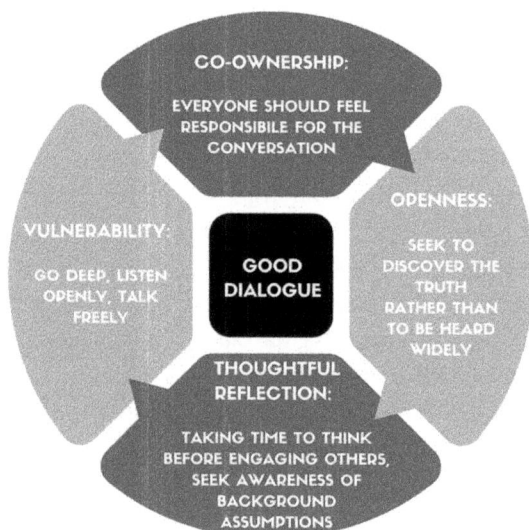

Figure 3.2. Good dialogue, including digital dialogue, requires the four following tenets: vulnerability, co-ownership, openness, and thoughtful reflection.

[12] Blaschko et al.

Vulnerability. When engaging others, it is important to cultivate a space where people can enter openly. To uncover the truth, one needs to bring their whole self to the conversation. Go deep: dig into the uncertain places where you might not know the answers. Listen actively, because others are sharing the space you are in. Achieving these things involves a willingness to refrain from debating with others—one that doesn't come without practice. We build vulnerability in the classroom in two key ways. First, we always show up to the classroom sharing our whole selves and not merely our academic selves. Second, we let students know when we do not know the answer to a question and invite them to do the same. We talk about what we agree with and what we find challenging. This helps pave the way for trust to build so that we can explore even harder spaces.

One way to think about vulnerability is as a bridge between people that needs to be crossed. Vulnerable information, therefore, is like a weight that must be carried while crossing that bridge. If you try to cross a footbridge with a heavy cart, the bridge might break. You need a strong enough structure to bear the weight of the vulnerable package crossing it. We build that bridge of trust by establishing a relationship with others. Bridges need to be built with work on both sides. Each person involved in a dialogue strengthens the structure by bringing him- or herself into that dialogue. By beginning with lighter topics and then turning to the weighty topics while checking in with one another, we build a bridge of trust. A stronger bridge of trust is needed to hold the weight of more serious or personal conversation—this is particularly important for online dialogue. Vulnerability also requires active listening—paying attention fully and listening to understand—and self-advocacy. To be vulnerable: go deep, listen openly, talk freely.

Co-ownership. Co-ownership (or egalitarianism) requires those entering dialogue to claim some ownership over the conversation. Everyone involved should feel a sense of responsibility over what transpires. It is important to make spaces comfortable to build vulnerability, which means everyone should take active ownership to make that happen. In digital spaces, anonymous or pseudonymous posting doesn't support co-ownership since it introduces distance into the relationship. This is especially problematic given the prevalence of Internet users who choose to use something other than their real identity online. Thus we have to actively work to support an experience of co-ownership among those entering into dialogue.

Openness. Here, again, we want to underline the importance of seeking truth rather than looking to be heard widely. To interact well with others and to learn from them, it is important to look for and identify differences and similarities in various ways of thinking that emanate from a dialogue group. This allows the group to form a foundation of shared interests or values, which will be built upon in the subsequent hard work of vulnerable dialogue. Likewise, it is equally important to identify differences between group members. As unique and individual humans, each of us has our own experiences that shape us. It is important to identify these differences in dialogue because it helps us see how and why the truth can look different to different people.

Let's return to the image of the statue. When two people are looking at the statue from opposite sides, they are going to see different features. This might lead to descriptions for what sounds like two entirely different objects. But in reality, it takes perhaps several people all looking from their unique perspectives at the same time to form a complete description of the statue. Dialogue is like this: we need to know that we are coming with unique perspectives as we approach a topic together. *Fratelli Tutti* reminds us that openness is a balance that requires a sense of identity grounded in culture and family: "I cannot truly encounter another unless I stand on firm foundations, for it is on the basis of these that I can accept the gift the other brings and in turn offer an authentic gift of my own" (143). Each unique perspective helps us uncover a unique side of the truth.

Something else to note here is that in discussing the different perspectives of a specific truth, it is important to understand that the virtue of openness is opposed to the vices of too much or too little openness. Too much openness means that we might lose track of the objectivity of truth, and too little means that we might lose track of the subjective experiences that reveal the nuances of the truth as well. If we have too much openness, we might agree to something being untrue when it is true, or we might affirm our partners' beliefs without adequately reflecting on what they had to say. Further, too little openness can lead to the types of counter-productive arguments that are all too common on social media. In such a scenario, the dialogue participants do not possess the necessary trust to be able to ask the "how?" and "why?" questions that will let them better understand one another. Openness requires a willingness to engage with others—a seeking out of differences to see how or why we have unique experiences that allow us to uncover the depth of the truth.

Thoughtful reflection. Finally, thoughtful reflection is required to have a truly meaningful dialogue experience that reaches the necessary depth of inquiry. When we engage others in conversation, we are able to go deep only when we have thoughtfully reflected on the topic. Social media platforms have encouraged surface-level engagement with information that is delivered swiftly and is immediately digestible. Twitter, with its character limit on posts that was widely imitated by other platforms, has gotten many of us in the habit of skimming a headline and thinking that we understand what it conveys when we do not. Moreover, feed-based platforms encourage an "immediate" response mentality that always fails to meaningfully engage with a topic.

Thoughtful reflection requires a bit of work to set up in a dialogue. We need to take the time to read, listen, and think before engaging others. Again, seeking background assumptions helps us to cast a critical eye, one that allows us to ask how and why this information is true, and what parts of it are merely a reflection of our position in the world. Being able to identify these features helps us to see ourselves more clearly and to identify our own biases and experiences that shape who we are.

Why Social Technology?

As we begin to think about our lives and the lives of others, it is important to consider what shapes our position in society. When we think about community and social interactions, it is easy to go directly to the roles people inhabit to shape the world around them. But society is made up of both the roles people take on and the people themselves. Philosophers of science and technology refer to these two domains as production (roles) and reproduction (people). Production and reproduction shape society and culture.[13] Technology can impact both production and reproduction. In this book we focus on technologies of production—social technologies —but note that there are just as many social concerns when it comes to reproductive technologies as well. Through reproduction, we create the next generation. Our only control over reproduction is who we choose to reproduce with—we cannot completely control our children or what happens to them in the world. Communication is more flexible and allows us to shape culture through the control of narrative. Social technologies provide many more openings to shape culture.

People are inherently social creatures. We live in communities and build norms for interacting with one another that lead to the formation of culture. Culture can change over time as some ideas fall out of fashion and others stand the test of time. Language plays a key role in this process. Take, for example, a hypothetical conversation with an older member of your family. In this conversation they say something that may seem jarring to you, perhaps even inappropriate. But, you must ask: "Is this intentional or merely a misinterpretation based on cultural norms established at a different point in time compared to the norms I am working from?" This can also happen when you visit a different country. First exposures

---

[13] Peter-Paul Verbeek, *Moralizing Technology: Understanding and Designing the Morality of Things* (Chicago: University of Chicago Press, 2011), https://press .uchicago.edu/ucp/books/book/chicago/M/bo11309162.html.

to new cultures can seem amazing or shocking. Your cultural context consists of community and communication.

Within any culture, digital tools for communication shape the way we interact. For example, when the authors of this book (Millennials) communicate with a younger generation (Gen Z), this usually occurs on video and photo-based applications like Snapchat or FaceTime. Rarely will that communication take place via a traditional phone call. However, phone calls are often the only way to reach members of an older generation (like the Silent Generation), who are more used to purely audio-based communication.[14]

Interestingly, the chosen medium of communication mediates what is discussed. The sharing of memes, videos, or emojis makes up the majority of the conversations on social media apps. At the same time, older adults who communicate only verbally often don't even know what a meme is. The purely audio-based medium is more constrained in terms of the communication styles it supports. This medium is also time-intensive because all information needs to be articulated verbally. A communicatory shortcut like a meme is a projection of the imagination that can convey an information-rich message in an instant. These differing styles of communication shape what we perceive to be important (how something looks versus how something sounds). Generational adherence to distinct modes of communication contributes to generational shifts in culture. Thus we can see how technology shapes culture in different ways across generations.

Commonly, when we think of technology, we think of it as a tool that allows us to perform a task. Sometimes it makes work easier (for example, the use of a hammer or electricity), and other times it facilitates entertainment (for example, a computer game or YouTube). Echoing Francis in *Laudato Si'*, technologies create social frameworks for society. We argue that any technology is not merely

---

[14] Shupei Yuan et al., "What Do They Like? Communication Preferences and Patterns of Older Adults in the United States: The Role of Technology," *Educational Gerontology* 42, no. 3 (October 2015).

a neutral tool but plays an active role in the ethics of the context in which it is used. This shapes culture. Technologies can make us more or less ethical. A few examples will help illustrate this.

Example 1: While they are not social technologies, speed bumps on roads provide an example for how technology can change our behaviors to allow or disallow certain actions to occur. Speed bumps do not merely *encourage* us to act more ethically, like the information shared from a screen-time tracker app. Speed bumps actually make it less possible to act unethically. They prohibit driving above the speed limit—if you drive over them at a high rate of speed, you will damage the bottom of your car. They do not merely suggest but induce the changed behavior, slowing down. Other forms of technology, including social technologies, can have similar effects: rather than merely providing information or making a suggestion, some technologies can shape the world and make a course of action either possible or impossible depending on the desired result.

Let's now connect the idea of the speed bump to the smartphone, which has fundamentally changed our day-to-day activities over the past decade. The excellent social benefit it provides, connecting us with the world, also comes with some negative aspects. One such negative aspect is the ease with which we can ignore what is happening around us in our physical proximity. This effect has a dual purpose. Sometimes this ability to step out of the physical world can make people thousands of miles apart feel much closer by allowing them to connect with one another. Other times it can make people sitting at the same dinner table feel farther apart when everyone is glued to their phones.

Example 2: Sensors such as phone cameras and microphones make it possible to have visual and audio data collected about you. Smartphones can also locate your position using GPS. If these pieces of technology were not integrated into your phone, companies could not collect and share large databases of personal information related to your behavior. While there are many benefits of a technology like GPS, such as avoiding getting lost and being easily able to find a new address, it comes with the inevitable effect of a third party being able to monitor your movements anywhere on the globe and subsequently sell that information to whoever is interested in it. When a social media platform uses all available sensors in a smartphone to harvest personal information, it establishes an exploitative relationship between the platform and its users.

Example 3: Consider how social media apps mediate how we perceive the world. Their algorithms and interfaces shape what we believe to be popular and current. Algorithms intentionally order content to guarantee that we see certain things first, making it appear that the content at the top of our feed is what is "popular" and worth consuming. They also determine what types of paid advertising we should see intermixed with non-paid posts in that same feed.

Now imagine that an audio-only social media app exists. How might that app shape what we perceive as being important through the content shared with us? It is possible that we would find a moan of pain more compelling than an exhaustive description of someone's injury. Without a picture to accompany the sound, we are left to interpret what the piece of software presents us with. A raw expression of pain would most likely prompt a higher emotional response than a dry verbal description. The type of information presented changes how we feel. Sounds of pain elicit more emotion and empathy than what we would get with purely curated visuals. So in this case both the algorithmic ordering and the content displayed communicate what is important to the users.

Social technologies can present a narrative about the world, and that narrative shapes the moral imagination of users consuming the content. The design of social technologies, thus, presents a moral choice: designers have power to shape the experience of users based on any decision they make. In considering the responsibility of developers, we'll discuss how Catholic Social Teaching can be used to set design principles for the creation of new and good social technologies in the rest of this book.

To Dialogue or Not to Dialogue?

Do we always need to engage in a dialogue when communicating online? Not necessarily. There are plenty of situations where a debate is actually appropriate, and others where we might just need a quick exchange of information. While we want to underline the importance of dialogue, we understand that sometimes only a thumbs-up emoji is needed on an "I'll meet you at 8pm" text message. But what if we want to have the option of entering into dialogue? The creation of a digital space that fosters dialogue requires the right settings, similar to how the speed bump slows drivers. Accordingly, we need features in our social technologies that direct users to enter into dialogue.

As we have emphasized, today's social technologies are largely built to keep the user online so that their attention can be monetized. What would it look like to build something directed toward the flourishing of the whole person? It would need to encourage and foster dialogue, especially in moments where the conversation moves beyond the surface level. How exactly can this be implemented? Read on to chapter 4 for how to begin building something that is genuinely good.

Chapter
FOUR

A Framework for Technology Design Based on Catholic Social Teaching

In the last chapter, we discussed the importance of good dialogue as a tool to bring us into deeper relationships with others. And while not every interaction transpiring online necessitates intentional dialogue, we want to ensure that it's always a possibility. How can we design social technologies for this? The answer is to use Catholic Social Teaching as our guide. The principles of Catholic Social Teaching will help us design social technologies that foster authentic dialogue and a number of other activities that are in accord with human flourishing and the common good.

But be forewarned: both this and the following chapter will provide a number of critiques of the technologies many of us know and use on a regular basis. We may criticize your favorite social media app (or even an app you rely on for your livelihood if you have an online business). We want to highlight that these are just that: critiques. If today's technologies were built in a way that was completely harmonious with Catholic Social Teaching, would we have social media platforms exactly like Instagram and TikTok? Almost certainly not. On the other hand, is it a sin to use Instagram and TikTok? Also no, as long as you are attempting to use them virtuously. In fact, because these social media platforms permeate so much of our life and culture today, it is important to have Catholic voices on them.

Here we propose a framework for social technology evaluation and design informed by the principles of Catholic Social Teaching. In software engineering, software design principles are the guiding rules that help software developers create programs that are organized, efficient, and easy to understand. With our proposed framework, we present software design principles that will orient the software toward human flourishing. This is in notable opposition to persuasive mechanisms: design decisions that give technologies power to encourage certain behaviors (like staying glued to your news feed) that often are not in accord with what is best for the human person.[1] Our framework sits between Catholic doctrine on human dignity and the common good, and software engineering principles for the design of new technology with some social component (see figure 1.2 in chapter 1). Before we outline the framework, we will first introduce and then expand on our method for analyzing the ethics of technology design and development.

The Think → Build → Do Sequence for Analyzing Technology

We learned in chapter 2 from Pope Benedict XVI and Pope Francis that technology is never neutral.[2] The technologies we build always reflect human values in their design. Over the course of the writing of this book, we, the authors, talked through the process of how different technologies are built to reflect different values and how the values underpinning a technology affect user behavior. In these conversations we realized we could distill the process of how values are embedded into technology and how

---

[1] Cennydd Bowles, *Future Ethics* (East Sussex, UK: NowNext Press, 2018), chap. 3.

[2] A number of scholars have argued this in a nonreligious context as well. In this book we've cited *Future Ethics* by Cennydd Bowles, *Technology and the Virtues* by Shannon Vallor, and *The Question Concerning Technology* by Martin Heidegger and William Lovitt, all of which argue that technology is not neutral.

those values in turn affect our lives into a simple sequence: Think → Build → Do. Let us explain this process further.

Think: Every company (or individual programmer) has core values that they have in mind when they are building their products. Even if their values aren't explicitly laid out, everyone has internal motivations for why they're building something. As an example, Facebook's core value is to connect the world.[3] They also highly prioritize user growth on the platform, which stems from Meta CEO Mark Zuckerberg's fear of Facebook becoming obsolete and irrelevant.[4] These values (and fears) shape the final product.

Build: How do these values come to life in a product? They come about through the platform's design of its user interface and user experience (UI/UX). User interface design pertains to the actual look of the product, including the design of its visual elements and touchpoints a person interacts with when using it. User experience design focuses on designing the entire experience a user has when interacting with a company and its products, including a product's usability, desirability, and brand perception. A product's combined user interface and user experience allows it to be used in particular ways. For example, Facebook's user interface and user experience design choices include the ability to make a profile and add friends, the ability to post to a news feed, the way the news feed algorithm ranks content in the feed, and even the product logo's particular shade of blue. As one example of how the "think" directly affects the "build," Facebook's news feed is designed to get people to spend more time on Facebook.[5] This approach stems from Facebook employees following the company's core value of trying to connect the world: in order for Facebook to effectively do that, people must use it regularly; thus Facebook designed its app to be habit-forming.[6]

[3] Sarah Frier, *No Filter: The Inside Story of Instagram* (New York: Simon and Schuster, 2020), 162.

[4] Frier, *No Filter*, 103, 124.

[5] Frier, 197.

[6] Frier, 162.

Do: How does a piece of software's design, which is influenced by the company's core values, affect user behavior? In the case of Facebook, a desire for increased user engagement led to a news feed design that boosted sensational content, which ultimately led to increased toxicity, including large amounts of angry comments and fighting on the site.[7] Social media apps like Facebook also changed the way we interact in social situations offline. The advent of the feed, photo albums, and "likes" caused people to focus on photographing their lives at the expense of enjoying social interactions in the present.

Our Catholic Social Teaching–based framework can come into play at both the "think" and the "do" stages: we can use it both to guide the design of new software as well as evaluate already-existing technologies. If someone wants to develop a new technology to promote the common good, they can consider the principles of Catholic Social Teaching in the "think" stage. For example, they could ask, how does this app promote the principle of *subsidiarity* or the *life and dignity of the human person*? If one wants to evaluate already-existing applications in light of Catholic Social Teaching, one can consider our framework in the "do" stage. For example, we can ask, does Facebook encourage users to act in a way that promotes their flourishing, and the flourishing of others? In the next section we will dive more deeply into eight main themes of Catholic Social Teaching, explaining each principle in more depth and outlining concretely how they can inform the design and evaluation of social technologies.

Eight Principles of Catholic Social Teaching Applied to Software Design

We will now outline our Catholic Social Teaching–based framework for the design and evaluation of social technologies. Our

---

[7] Keach Hagey and Jeff Horwitz, "Facebook Tried to Make Its Platform a Healthier Place. It Got Angrier Instead," *Wall Street Journal*, September 2021, https://www.wsj.com/articles/facebook-algorithm-change-zuckerberg-11631654215.

framework takes eight of the main principles of Catholic Social Teaching—*life and dignity of the human person; call to family, community, and participation; rights and responsibilities; option for the poor and vulnerable; dignity of work and rights of workers; solidarity; subsidiarity; and care for God's creation*—and makes suggestions for software design according to them.

1. Life and Dignity of the Human Person:

> *We believe that every person is precious, that people are more important than things, and that the measure of every institution is whether it threatens or enhances the life and dignity of the human person.*[8]

In the first chapter, we considered Shannon Vallor's concern that many social technologies make it harder to exercise self-control compared to other tools, technological or not. Many of the addictive mechanisms of social technologies come from how social media companies monetize our attention.[9] Monetizing our attention prioritizes excess profits over the good of the human person—a violation of human dignity.

We also discussed Francis's observation in *Fratelli Tutti* that current social technologies foster parallel monologues rather than authentic dialogue (200), and we compared that to Vallor's concern about how frictionless interactions prevent people from building the virtue required to maintain meaningful relationships.[10] When we cultivate habits of communication shaped by today's social technologies, we may end up lacking the ability to affirm the dignity of others through careful listening to their points of view and

---

[8] United States Conference of Catholic Bishops, "Seven Themes of Catholic Social Teaching."

[9] Hiniker and Wobbrock, "Reclaiming Attention," 40–44.

[10] Vallor, *Technology and the Virtues*, sec. 7.1.1.

to cultivate empathy toward them even if we disagree with their beliefs.[11]

This connects to social media's tendency to promote homogeneity of thought. A common example of the homogeneity of thought found on social media is when someone posts a controversial or minority opinion on Twitter and is verbally silenced by the "Twitter mob." Though this sort of behavior could happen in real life, it is more likely to be encouraged by the design of an online platform like Twitter where many users can easily gather and where they may not see the humanity of the person they're attacking as effectively when they are behind a screen. Vallor points out that such constant surveillance of people's opinions may work too well in forcing us to act "rightly" in the short term, sacrificing the moral and cultural "play" required for the maturation of selves and communities.[12] Vallor says, "Perhaps becoming or remaining 'civilized' requires that I enjoy some creative license to experiment with thought and action in arenas that are not immediately subject to judgment by others, especially when those 'others' represent the cultural status quo."[13]

In order for social technologies to foster such moral "play," they must be designed in such a way that users are provided with private spaces for moral exploration with a few trusted friends, along with healthy guidelines and moderation when discussing contentious issues with a wider sphere. A study on hard conversations in online spaces found that study participants often preferred to discuss controversial topics in private or in audience-restricted online spaces, corroborating Vallor's idea.[14]

Another example of how social media platforms promote homogeneity of thought is through their medium of short-form posts. Although most social media platforms don't enforce as hard of a

---

[11] Samuel, "It's Hard to Be a Moral Person."
[12] Vallor, *Technology and the Virtues*, 191.
[13] Vallor, 191.
[14] Baughan et al., "Someone Is Wrong on the Internet," 1–22.

character limit as Twitter does (280 characters for free or more for a price), content on social media tends to be shorter-form because of space limitations, aesthetics, or the need to communicate quickly. While there are benefits to this, the downside is that it forces nuanced ideas to be communicated in a way that is too succinct to capture their depth. These ideas are often communicated in a catchy and attractive way that encourages people to just accept the idea as fact rather than to enter into a rich dialogue with it. In this way, homogeneity of thought is promoted further.

With all of this in mind, the design principles for social technologies that we propose from the *Life and Dignity of the Human Person* principle of Catholic Social Teaching can be seen in figure 4.1.

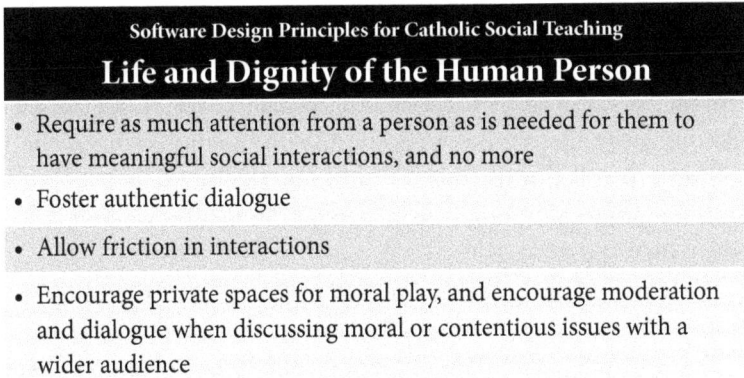

Software Design Principles for Catholic Social Teaching
Life and Dignity of the Human Person

- Require as much attention from a person as is needed for them to have meaningful social interactions, and no more
- Foster authentic dialogue
- Allow friction in interactions
- Encourage private spaces for moral play, and encourage moderation and dialogue when discussing moral or contentious issues with a wider audience

Figure 4.1. Design principles for social technologies that we propose from the *Life and Dignity of the Human Person* principle of Catholic Social Teaching.

2. *Call to Family, Community, and Participation:*

> *The person is not only sacred but also social. How we organize our society—in economics and politics, in law and policy— directly affects human dignity and the capacity of individuals to grow in community. Marriage and the family are the central social institutions that must be supported and strengthened, not*

*undermined. We believe people have a right and a duty to par-
ticipate in society, seeking together the common good and well-
being of all, especially the poor and vulnerable.*[15]

A clear benefit of social technologies is that they enable efficient
communication from afar. This has a number of benefits for bringing families and communities together. We are able to connect with
family and friends we are physically separated from through updates on social media, texting, and video chatting. Similarly, we
can now collaborate with colleagues in distant places and find community online with people who may share our niche hobbies or
unique experiences. In this vein, Benedict XVI praised the Internet
for its ability to connect isolated Christians with one another.[16] In
crisis situations when gathering in person is more difficult—for
example, during the COVID-19 pandemic before vaccines and
effective medical treatments were available—social technologies
provided a safe avenue for social interaction. Even though social
technologies help us grow in community in situations where meeting in person is not feasible, Francis has reminded us in *Fratelli
Tutti* that they cannot replace in-person interaction when it is appropriate or possible (43).

We learned during the COVID-19 pandemic that spending too
much time per day on video calls can make us feel exhausted and
anxious, which led to a phenomenon called Zoom Fatigue.[17] According to a Pew Research study on the online habits of Americans
during the COVID-19 pandemic, 68 percent of Americans said
that while digital interactions were useful, they could not replace

[15] United States Conference of Catholic Bishops, "Seven Themes of Catholic Social Teaching."

[16] Pope Benedict XVI, "47th World Communications Day."

[17] Ryan W. Miller, "What's 'Zoom Fatigue'? Here's Why Video Calls Can Be So Exhausting," *USA Today*, April 23, 2020, https://www.usatoday.com/story/news/nation/2020/04/23/zoom-fatigue-video-calls-coronavirus-can-make-us-tired-anxious/3010478001/.

in-person interactions.[18] Furthermore, there is evidence that friendships forged offline are usually stronger than friendships made online.[19] While social technologies are useful, it would be detrimental to our well-being if they replaced in-person interactions in situations where meeting in person is feasible.

We just discussed how technology usage can impact our ability to grow in community. We now want to discuss another aspect of the call to family, community, and participation: how community participation in design processes can help to build technologies that serve more people more effectively. The Design Justice movement in computer science advocates for such community participation in design processes, noting that "the people who are most adversely affected by design decisions—about visual culture, new technologies, the planning of our communities, or the structure of our political and economic systems—tend to have the least influence on those decisions and how they are made."[20] As an example, someone with darker skin may struggle to use the fun augmented-reality facial filters built into Snapchat, Instagram, and TikTok if those filters are calibrated to detect faces with lighter skin. When people from different backgrounds and experiences are included in the design process, they will design technological solutions that work for more people, and those people will feel their human dignity affirmed.

The design principles we propose for *Call to Family, Community, and Participation* are seen in figure 4.2.

[18] Colleen McClain et al., "How the Internet and Technology Shaped Americans' Personal Experiences amid COVID-19," Pew Research Center: Internet, Science & Tech, April 2022, https://www.pewresearch.org/internet/2021/09/01/how-the-internet-and-technology-shaped-americans-personal-experiences-amid-covid-19/.

[19] Darius K-S Chan and Grand H-L Cheng, "A Comparison of Offline and Online Friendship Qualities at Different Stages of Relationship Development," *Journal of Social and Personal Relationships* 21, no. 3 (2004): 305–20.

[20] "Design Justice Network Principles," Design Justice Network, 2018, https://designjustice.org/read-the-principles. While we acknowledge that some of the beliefs of the Design Justice movement are not harmonious with a Catholic worldview, we appreciate and can learn from the good elements of the movement.

Software Design Principles for Catholic Social Teaching

Call to Family, Community, and Participation

- Do not build social technologies that have the goal of replacing in-person interactions

- Social technologies are at the service of fostering stronger connections between families and communities

- Involve members of the community, especially those on the margins of society, in the design process

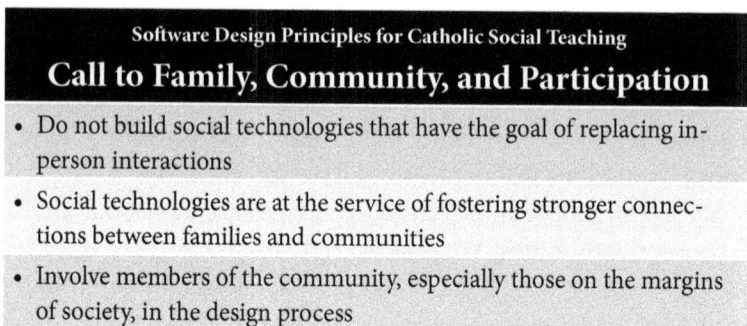

Figure 4.2. Design principles for social technologies that we propose from the *Call to Family, Community, and Participation* principle of Catholic Social Teaching.

3. Rights and Responsibilities:

> *The Catholic tradition teaches that human dignity can be protected and a healthy community can be achieved only if human rights are protected and responsibilities are met. Therefore, every person has a fundamental right to life and a right to those things required for human decency. Corresponding to these rights are duties and responsibilities—to one another, to our families, and to the larger society.*[21]

In the interest of promoting innovation, the government in the United States has refrained from tightly regulating technology companies.[22] A lack of regulation means that instead of democratically elected officials deciding how technology will affect us, those decisions are left to the Silicon Valley C-suite executives. More likely than not, these executives will make decisions based on what is best for their business rather than what is best for their users. Furthermore, these executives lack the legitimacy to make such

---

[21] United States Conference of Catholic Bishops, "Seven Themes of Catholic Social Teaching."

[22] Reich, Sahami, and Weinstein, *System Error*, chap. 3.

sweeping decisions about our lives that elected officials have earned through democratic elections.[23]

Currently, social technology companies make no meaningful promises to protect the dignity of their users or the good of society. The ubiquity of social technologies in modern society and the lack of regulation necessitates a social contract between these companies and their users. This would ensure that companies will act in the best interest of users and establish tech executives as legitimate authorities over decisions that affect the day-to-day life of ordinary people in a profound way. Social technology companies must acknowledge the responsibility they have toward their users.

As an example, many social media companies today violate human rights when they harvest and monetize our personal thoughts. Catholic legal scholar Evelyn Aswad argues that to fully protect human dignity we must acknowledge that we have the right to hold opinions without interference, and that many Internet companies today violate this right. The freedom to form and hold opinions has three dimensions: the right not to be compelled into revealing your opinions, the right not to be penalized for your inner thoughts, and the right not to be manipulated in the formation of your opinions. Aswad argues that business models that collect our data and profit from it (a key business strategy employed by many social media platforms in order to make their services "free" to users) violate the freedom to form and hold opinions. Companies do this by using computational techniques to analyze our personal data to tell what we're thinking. That data is then used to discriminate among consumers, showing them different ads or information based on their perceived tastes, possibly even swaying opinions through targeted information.[24]

In response to all of these problems, the design principle we propose for *Rights and Responsibilities* can be found in figure 4.3.

---

[23] Reich, Sahami, and Weinstein, *System Error*, 67–68.
[24] Evelyn Aswad, "Losing the Freedom to Be Human," *Columbia Human Rights Law Review* 52 (February 29, 2020).

Software Design Principles for Catholic Social Teaching
Rights and Responsibilities
• Establish a social contract between social technology companies and users that doesn't leave one group advantaged over the other

Figure 4.3. Design principle for social technologies that we propose for the *Rights and Responsibilities* principle of Catholic Social Teaching.

4. *Option for the Poor and Vulnerable:*

> *A basic moral test is how our most vulnerable members are faring. In a society marred by deepening divisions between rich and poor, our tradition recalls the story of the Last Judgment (Mt 25:31-46) and instructs us to put the needs of the poor and vulnerable first.*[25]

Currently, we tend to think of the poor and vulnerable as those experiencing material poverty, or those marginalized or discriminated against because of some aspect of their identity, for example, racial- or gender-based discrimination. However, we propose that in addition to amplifying the systemic injustices present in society, technology expands vulnerability to a wider population. In terms of relationship-building, social technologies have made us all potentially vulnerable to cyberbullying, trolling, and politically charged verbal attacks.

Additionally, social media addiction is something we all find ourselves vulnerable to. Today, social media users are exploited at the hands of technology executives whose advertising-based profit models incentivize social media apps to do anything they can to capture attention for as long as possible. Inflammatory interactions fix our attention more than respectful ones, so social media companies design subtle nudges toward hostile interactions into their

---

[25] United States Conference of Catholic Bishops, "Seven Themes of Catholic Social Teaching."

applications to keep us engaged for longer periods of time.[26] Thus for the issues of both relationship-building and addiction, we find ourselves exploited at the hands of technology companies attempting to maximize their profits. This is reminiscent of the factory workers of the Industrial Revolution, who were exploited by greedy factory owners who instituted unfair working conditions to maximize profits. In both cases, excess profit comes before respect for human dignity.

But of course, Catholic Social Teaching tells us that some amount of profit is useful and important to promote the health of a business. The issue is that when profit becomes the exclusive goal of a business, it can become destructive (*Caritas in Veritate* 21; *Populorum Progressio* 26). In their book *Counting the Cost*, Clemens Sedmak and Kelli Reagan Hickey propose non-maximization as one principle Catholic institutions should follow in their budgeting practices. They note that "the idea of maximization implies a human tendency to strive for more, often without limit. In other words, there is no saturation point—there can always be more wealth, more goods, more profit."[27]

There are examples of the principle of non-maximization being modeled well in the Catholic world. In 2019, the Carthusian monks in France, makers of the Chartreuse liqueur, decided to scale back their production in order to allow themselves more time for prayer and to limit the environmental impact of Chartreuse production.[28] Rather than focusing on limitless growth, the Carthusians put a limit on their production that would have a positive impact on both the monks (more time for prayer) and the world (helping to care for the environment). Can technology companies similarly follow

---

[26] Hagey and Horwitz, "Facebook Tried to Make Its Platform a Healthier Place."

[27] Clemens Sedmak and Kelli Reagan Hickey, *Counting the Cost: Financial Decision-Making, Discipleship, and Christian Living*, Enacting Catholic Social Tradition (Collegeville, MN: Liturgical Press, 2023), 151.

[28] Becky Cooper, "Why Is Chartreuse Hard to Find Right Now? Ask the Monks Who Make It," *New York Times*, April 14, 2023, sec. Food, https://www.nytimes.com/2023/04/14/dining/drinks/chartreuse-shortage.html.

this principle? The firm Anchor Group operates in this way. Founded as a Catholic technology consultancy that helps Christian men develop themselves through their work, Anchor Group promotes healthy working hours, has structured times of prayer and formation throughout the workday, and, in line with the principles of Catholic Social Teaching, prioritizes the well-being of its employees over profit.[29]

Thus far we've used an expansive definition of "poor and vulnerable" that is not restricted to just the materially poor and vulnerable. However, we of course cannot forget about the materially poor! As it turns out, the attention economy can have a negative effect on the materially poor through the way consumeristic habits of the wealthy negatively affect the poor. In the late 1980s, John Paul II criticized the culture of superdevelopment, "which consists in an excessive availability of every kind of material goods for the benefit of certain social groups [and] easily makes people slaves of 'possession' and of immediate gratification" (*Sollicitudo Rei Socialis* 28). The advertising-based profit model of the attention economy that is employed on social media brings the consumeristic mindset of superdevelopment to everyone's fingertips. Not only is adopting a consumeristic mindset detrimental to one's spiritual life, but Catholic Social Teaching also tells us that consumeristic tendencies of the wealthy negatively impact the poor (*Sollicitudo Rei Socialis* 28). In the way that the consumeristic tendencies of the wealthy harm the poor, and that the attention economy promotes consumerism, the attention economy hurts the poor.

In *Sollicitudo Rei Socialis* John Paul II also proposes that solidarity with people who are socioeconomically marginalized is a key to fighting the greed and lust for power that are symptomatic of a culture of superdevelopment. As such, we can return to the notion of Design Justice, which we mentioned in relation to the call to family, community, and participation. Can we additionally include

---

[29] Julian Kwasniewski, "A Catholic Workspace," *Crisis Magazine*, August 12, 2023, https://crisismagazine.com/opinion/a-catholic-workspace.

the poor in our design processes? If yes, then we better address their needs and temper the excessive habits of society at large.

The design principles we propose for *Option for the Poor and Vulnerable* can be found in figure 4.4.

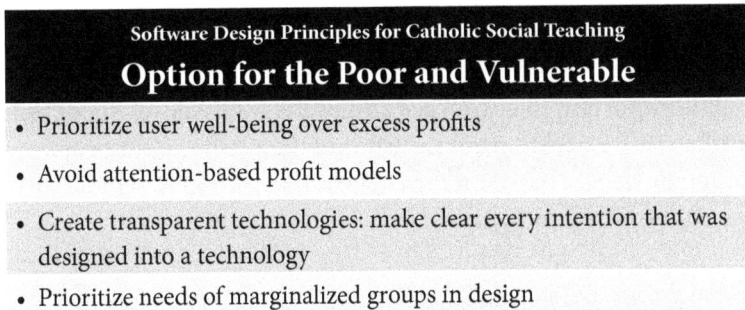

Software Design Principles for Catholic Social Teaching

Option for the Poor and Vulnerable

- Prioritize user well-being over excess profits

- Avoid attention-based profit models

- Create transparent technologies: make clear every intention that was designed into a technology

- Prioritize needs of marginalized groups in design

Figure 4.4. Design principles for social technologies that we propose from the *Option for the Poor and Vulnerable* principle of Catholic Social Teaching.

5. *The Dignity of Work and the Rights of Workers:*

> *The economy must serve people, not the other way around. Work is more than a way to make a living; it is a form of continuing participation in God's creation. If the dignity of work is to be protected, then the basic rights of workers must be respected—the right to productive work, to decent and fair wages, to the organization and joining of unions, to private property, and to economic initiative.*[30]

This principle has less to do with the social technology apps themselves and more with the well-being of those developing the apps. Silicon Valley has increasingly celebrated a culture of over-work, with some tech entrepreneurs encouraging eighteen-hour

---

[30] United States Conference of Catholic Bishops, "Seven Themes of Catholic Social Teaching."

workdays. This culture has led employees to neglect their families and even to commit suicide.[31] Contrasting today's work culture to that of the Industrial Revolution, the journalist Dan Lyons writes, "A century ago, factory workers were forming unions and going on strike to demand better conditions and a limit on hours. Today, Silicon Valley employees celebrate their own exploitation."[32] However, overworking leads to misery,[33] declining health,[34] and, ironically, decreased productivity.[35]

It is important to encourage and protect the well-being of tech workers as we benefit from the fruits of their labors. Our proposed design principles based on the *Dignity of Work and Rights of Workers* can be found in figure 4.5.

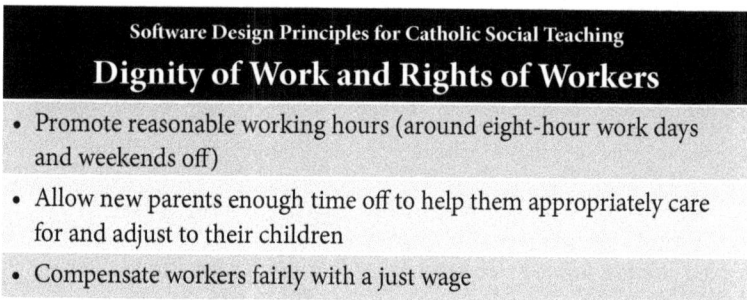

Software Design Principles for Catholic Social Teaching

Dignity of Work and Rights of Workers

- Promote reasonable working hours (around eight-hour work days and weekends off)
- Allow new parents enough time off to help them appropriately care for and adjust to their children
- Compensate workers fairly with a just wage

Figure 4.5. Design principles for social technologies that we propose for the *Dignity of Work and Rights of Workers* principle of Catholic Social Teaching.

[31] Dan Lyons, "In Silicon Valley, Working 9 to 5 Is for Losers," *New York Times*, August 31, 2017, https://www.nytimes.com/2017/08/31/opinion/sunday/silicon-valley-work-life-balance-.html.

[32] Lyons.

[33] Derek Thompson, "Workism Is Making Americans Miserable," *The Atlantic*, February 24, 2019, https://www.theatlantic.com/ideas/archive/2019/02/religion-workism-making-americans-miserable/583441/.

[34] Amanda Ruggeri, "The Compelling Case for Working a Lot Less," *BBC Worklife*, December 4, 2017, https://www.bbc.com/worklife/article/20171204-the-compelling-case-for-working-a-lot-less.

[35] Ruggeri; José Luis Peñarredonda, "What Happens When We Work Non-Stop," *BBC Worklife*, August 23, 2018, https://www.bbc.com/worklife/article/20180823-how-bad-for-you-is-working-non-stop.

6. *Solidarity:*

> *Our love for all our sisters and brothers demands that we pro-*
> *mote peace in a world surrounded by violence and conflict.*[36]

The principle of solidarity requires that we show concern for all people struggling throughout the world. As Francis notes, "The Internet, in particular, offers immense possibilities for encounter and solidarity. This is something truly good, a gift from God."[37] Through the Internet, we are better able to encounter the world's problems than ever before. With the advent of social media, victims of war and oppression have a greater ability to share their experiences with a mass audience. Even before the Internet, in the 1960s, the Vatican was aware that new technologies were enabling us to maintain more social connections, and it recognized through the documents of Catholic Social Teaching that this greater number of social connections necessitated a greater responsibility for one another (*Mater et Magistra* 62; *Pacem in Terris* 130).

However, Vallor notes two common pitfalls with Internet activism. The first is that our increased exposure to tragic situations can cause an empathic overload that ultimately leads to withdrawal and apathy rather than action. The second is that online activism runs the risk of being reduced to a "viral social meme with a shelf life far shorter than the social need."[38] Consonant with this is the *slacktivism* phenomenon. Slacktivism is when someone believes they have participated significantly in supporting a cause after performing a low-effort action like signing a petition or sharing a post on social media.[39] Its pitfall is that it fosters a mindset that one is doing more than they actually are, thereby limiting one's desire and potential to perform larger and more meaningful activism.

---

[36] United States Conference of Catholic Bishops, "Seven Themes of Catholic Social Teaching."

[37] Pope Francis, "Message for the 2014 World Communications Day," 113.

[38] Vallor, *Technology and the Virtues*, 172.

[39] Vallor, 172.

Responding to these problems, the design principles we propose for *Solidarity* can be found in figure 4.6.

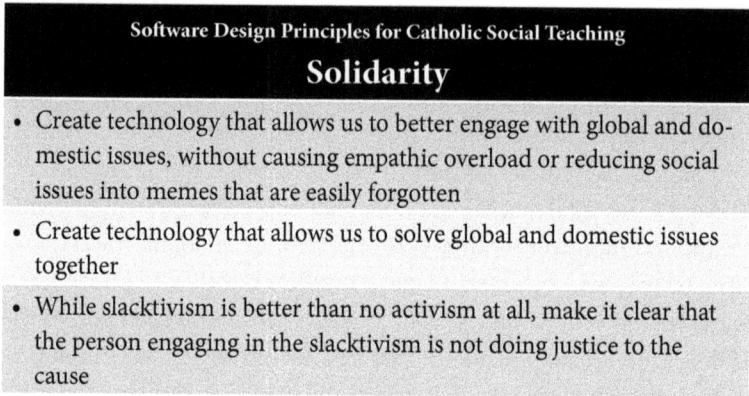

Software Design Principles for Catholic Social Teaching
Solidarity
• Create technology that allows us to better engage with global and domestic issues, without causing empathic overload or reducing social issues into memes that are easily forgotten
• Create technology that allows us to solve global and domestic issues together
• While slacktivism is better than no activism at all, make it clear that the person engaging in the slacktivism is not doing justice to the cause

Figure 4.6. Design principles for social technologies that we propose for the *Solidarity* principle of Catholic Social Teaching.

7. Subsidiarity:

> *According to the principle of subsidiarity, decisions should be made at the lowest level possible and the highest level necessary. Subsidiarity is crucial because it has applications in just about every aspect of moral life. In medical ethics, subsidiarity helps guide decision-making. In social ethics, subsidiarity helps us prudentially judge not only decision-making but allocation of resources. Subsidiarity is an effort at balancing the many necessary levels of society—and at its best, the principle of subsidiarity navigates the allocation of resources by higher levels of society to support engagement and decision-making by the lower levels.*[40]

The principle of subsidiarity advocates that decisions be made at the lowest level of governance possible. This affirms the dignity

[40] Meghan Clark, "Subsidiarity Is a Two-Sided Coin," Catholic Moral Theology, March 8, 2012, https://catholicmoraltheology.com/subsidiarity-is-a-two-sided-coin/.

of every individual involved in the decision-making process by trusting those at the local level to make good decisions and exercise their agency, creativity, and judgment rather than being micromanaged from above. In the words of Benedict XVI, "Subsidiarity respects personal dignity by recognizing in the person a subject who is always capable of giving something to others" (*Caritas in Veritate* 57). At the same time, the principle of subsidiarity recognizes the importance of the intervention of higher levels of society when needed. However, this intervention should be in a way that offers support that allows the lower levels of society to thrive.

In order for the lower levels of governance to be effective, citizens must be engaged in their local communities.[41] How can our social technologies foster the civic engagement required for healthy societies? A challenge to answering this question has been the alienating effect of social media use on users, which leads to a second, related question: How can our social technologies foster authentic community rather than isolation behind computer screens?

Today's social technologies allow us to maintain more relationships than we were ever able to in the pre-Internet era. This can be a wonderful thing when it allows us to stay connected with family and friends and connect with like-minded people who we otherwise wouldn't have met. There are even Catholic *influencers* (digital creators who have amassed large social media followings) who met their spouses through Twitter and Instagram![42] The large number of connections social media affords can also be a blessing when injustices are able to be seen and heard across the globe and petitions and fundraising materials for worthy causes are able to be shared widely. At the same time, we must be careful to not connect with so many people online that it degrades our capacity to engage deeply with our local communities.

---

[41] Tim Lanigan, "Catholic Social Teaching: Subsidiarity," For Your Marriage, accessed July 20, 2023, https://www.foryourmarriage.org/catholic-social-teaching-subsidiarity/.

[42] One example: https://www.instagram.com/p/CDH3pwHH1Zp/.

It is common to follow both distant acquaintances and influencers we don't know personally. We end up learning a lot about the lives of strangers, to an extent that may not be helpful for us. It may be going too far to say it's a grave sin to view posts from an old childhood acquaintance on Instagram, yet at the same time we must stop and ask ourselves: "If I'm never going to speak to this person again, is it really helpful and productive to be snooping into their life?" More often than not, viewing the content of either influencers or old acquaintances who we're not in touch with anymore just serves our own amusement and unvirtuous curiosity. On the other hand, viewing online snapshots of the lives of people with whom we are still in touch can strengthen our relationship with them.[43]

We are not necessarily recommending that all connections on the Internet must be with people one knows in real life. Our recommendation here is that the more social media fosters small group interactions and authentic connection rather than connects colossal groups of strangers, the more it will help foster the participation in community life that is necessary for a healthy society.

At the service of this goal is considering how subsidiarity can additionally inform our approach to content moderation and participation. The principle of subsidiarity is first and foremost about allowing people at the most local levels to participate in decision-making when appropriate. Social media platforms like Facebook, Instagram, and Twitter make all of the decisions pertaining to user experience from the top down. This means that all users of these platforms are subject to the same persuasive design principles coded into the platforms to make money while eroding civility. A better way forward is for software developers to think critically about the goal of their product and how much top-down influence is required for the product to work toward it. One way to imple-

---

[43] Monica Anderson et al., "Connection, Creativity and Drama: Teen Life on Social Media in 2022," Pew Research Center, November 16, 2022, https://www .pewresearch.org/internet/2022/11/16/connection-creativity-and-drama-teen -life-on-social-media-in-2022/.

ment the principle of subsidiarity in social technologies is to allow users to self-moderate their conversations when possible or prudent. One example of this could be a Discord server for a particular special interest that's limited to a small number of users who vote on and self-enforce their moderation guidelines. Of course, depending on the context, moderation from a higher level may be necessary to make the site work well.

An example of this is the platform Reddit. Although we primarily advocate for small-group interactions for social technologies, Reddit is an example of a social technology where it can be beneficial to have a wider audience. Of course, a lot of the conversations on Reddit are antisocial.[44] However, some corners of Reddit can be incredibly beneficial, and especially benefit from having a wider audience. One example of this is someone desiring to change the oil in their car themselves for the first time and looking for advice relating to their car's make and model on its individual subreddit. While this use of Reddit benefits from a wider audience, an audience of this size is also an invitation to a more top-down style of moderation because individual participants may be less invested in keeping the conversation respectful in a larger and more impersonal group. In fact, Reddit does implement a top-down approach to moderation by having designated moderators for different subreddits. These moderators enforce community rules, mediate disputes, ensure discussions remain on topic, and remove posts (and users!) that do not adhere to the community guidelines for that particular subreddit.

Another way the principle of subsidiarity could be implemented is through *open-source software*. Open-source software is software that comes bundled with its source code so users can customize the program to their liking. Open-source code could help promote the principle of subsidiarity in social technologies by providing

---

[44] Christine Lagorio-Chafkin, *We Are the Nerds: The Birth and Tumultuous Life of Reddit, the Internet's Culture Laboratory*, illustrated ed. (New York: Hachette Books, 2018).

the source code for a base platform that enables social communication, but allowing users to modify it to their liking to enable the features that best support their communities.

The design principles we propose for *Subsidiarity* are found in figure 4.7:

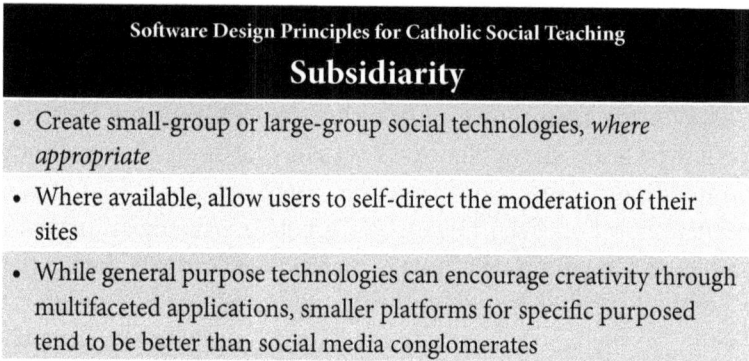

Software Design Principles for Catholic Social Teaching
Subsidiarity
• Create small-group or large-group social technologies, *where appropriate*
• Where available, allow users to self-direct the moderation of their sites
• While general purpose technologies can encourage creativity through multifaceted applications, smaller platforms for specific purposed tend to be better than social media conglomerates

Figure 4.7. Design principles for social technologies that we propose for the *Subsidiarity* principle of Catholic Social Teaching.

8. *Care for God's Creation:*

> We show our respect for the Creator by our stewardship of creation. Care for the earth is not just an Earth Day slogan, it is a requirement of our faith. We are called to protect people and the planet, living our faith in relationship with all of God's creation. This environmental challenge has fundamental moral and ethical dimensions that cannot be ignored.[45]

Recall that in their exploration of Christian relationship-based technology design, Hiniker and Wobbrock discussed how technology can assist our relationships not only with God and with others

---

[45] United States Conference of Catholic Bishops, "Seven Themes of Catholic Social Teaching."

but also with creation.[46] Alienation and addiction caused by social technology usage can cause people to turn inward and become wrapped up in a completely digital world, losing their sense of wonder for the natural world. When one loses their sense of wonder of nature, how can they be motivated to steward the environment? This does not have to be the case—technology could have an explicitly positive impact on the environment. There is promise that mobile applications can be designed to intentionally lead people to a deeper relationship with nature, including promoting a deeper appreciation of one's natural surroundings and encouraging conversations about nature.[47]

Additionally, we discussed the drawbacks of advertising-based profit models, including leading people into social media addiction and promoting consumeristic mindsets that hurt both the consumer and the poor. The advertising-based model has another drawback: leading people into overconsumption, which in turn is bad for the environment. Employing different profit models for social technologies—for example, subscription-based profit models or tiered pricing models—could ensure that social technology usage does not inadvertently lead to environmental harm through superfluous advertising.

Another environmental impact of technology pertains to the devices themselves. Modern smartphones have an unsustainable environmental impact: they are built with irreplaceable elements, contribute to deforestation in the Amazon, generate more greenhouse gasses than any other consumer electronic device, and generate toxic waste when not properly recycled.[48] While we should advocate for smartphones to be developed more sustainably, the

---

[46] Hiniker and Wobbrock, "Reclaiming Attention."

[47] Saba Kawas et al., "NatureCollections: Can a Mobile Application Trigger Children's Interest in Nature?," in *CSEDU* 1 (2020): 579–92.

[48] Bruno Martín, "The Hidden Environmental Toll of Smartphones," *OpenMind*, BBVA, February 24, 2020, https://www.bbvaopenmind.com/en/science/environment/the-hidden-environmental-toll-of-smartphones/.

environment also benefits from our exercising temperance in purchasing the latest device.

The backend infrastructure powering our social technologies behind the scenes has an environmental impact as well. Data centers consume a detrimental amount of energy,[49] and virtual environments at the scale of the nascent metaverse have the potential for significant environmental cost.[50] Care must be taken to evaluate the benefits of the technology being built versus its environmental cost.

The design principles we propose for *Care for God's Creation* can be found in figure 4.8:

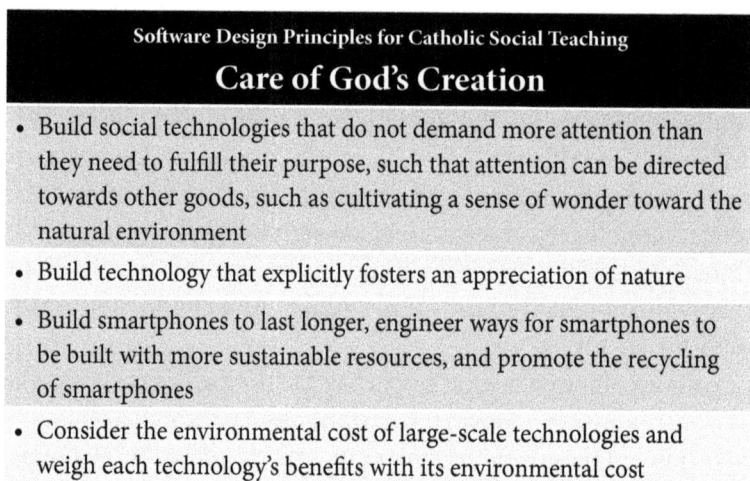

Software Design Principles for Catholic Social Teaching

Care of God's Creation

- Build social technologies that do not demand more attention than they need to fulfill their purpose, such that attention can be directed towards other goods, such as cultivating a sense of wonder toward the natural environment

- Build technology that explicitly fosters an appreciation of nature

- Build smartphones to last longer, engineer ways for smartphones to be built with more sustainable resources, and promote the recycling of smartphones

- Consider the environmental cost of large-scale technologies and weigh each technology's benefits with its environmental cost

---

Figure 4.8. Design principles for social technologies that we propose for the *Care for God's Creation* principle of Catholic Social Teaching.

---

[49] Mark Labbe, "Energy Consumption of AI Poses Environmental Problems," *SearchEnterpriseAI*, TechTarget, August 26, 2021, https://www.techtarget.com/searchenterpriseai/feature/Energy-consumption-of-AI-poses-environmental-problems; Carole-Jean Wu et al., "Sustainable AI: Environmental Implications, Challenges and Opportunities," *Proceedings of Machine Learning and Systems* 4 (2022): 795–813.

[50] Rachel Cross, "The Metaverse: Environmental Costs of Virtual Reality," *Impakter*, June 1, 2022, https://impakter.com/the-metaverse-environmental-costs-of-virtual-reality/.

Applying the Framework

A product's design determines what things we can (and can't) do with it. A product may even be designed *persuasively*, in ways that nudge us toward certain behaviors. Instead of design that persuades us to act in ways that make excess profit for Silicon Valley at the expense of our human flourishing, can we design technology that persuades us toward virtue and the common good?[51] The principles of Catholic Social Teaching can help inspire such technological designs.

We hope that our Catholic Social Teaching–based software design framework will guide the development of technology at the early stages. In addition to guiding the development of new technologies, the framework can also be used to evaluate platforms that already exist. In the next chapter we will outline case studies from the realm of online Catholic communities to analyze how they fare in light of Catholic Social Teaching. We hope that viewing these platforms through the lens of Catholic Social Teaching will help us to see which aspects of the social media platforms we use every day contribute to our flourishing and which aspects hinder it.

[51] Bowles, *Future Ethics*, 57–58.

Chapter FIVE

Case Studies

In this chapter, we look at four different cases where the Catholic world has interfaced in some way with the Internet. These cases are varied, such that they reflect the use of existing platforms developed in a purely secular context, as well as homegrown software that was developed with a specific Catholic mission in mind. Of course, we care about everyone's well-being on online platforms, regardless of whether or not they are Catholic. We also hope that any future technologies designed using our Catholic Social Teaching–based framework will benefit everyone, not just Catholics. However, in this chapter we are particularly interested in reflecting on the behavior of Catholics on different platforms because, in committing oneself to practicing the Catholic faith, one should strive to practice virtue and live out the principles of Catholic Social Teaching to the extent they are able.

In each case, we apply the framework introduced in chapter 4 to filter the software through the lens of Catholic Social Teaching. This analysis follows our core sequence of Think → Build → Do. In the "Think" component of the analysis, we scrutinize the design of the software as originally conceived. In the "Build" component of the analysis, we look at how the software was actually implemented, and how, in some cases, that implementation deviated from the original ideas. In the "Do" component of the analysis, the activities of the users are matched to specific Catholic Social Teaching principles. Interestingly, we show here how secular designs collide with Catholic use and how Catholic designs sometimes stray from the intentions of Catholic teaching. Our expectation isn't perfection—there is some good in all of these things, in spite of the occasional (or maybe frequent) misstep. There is also much to learn for the design of even better technologies.

Case Study 1: "Catholic Twitter"

Twitter was an early and enduring hangout spot for Catholics online. A loose community formed over time with a motley assortment of active participants, from famous journalists (e.g., Ross Douthat [@DouthatNYT], Elizabeth Bruenig [@ebruenig]) to pseudonymous posters with comparably large followings (e.g., "Woke Space Jesuit" [@MadocCairns], "Common Catholic Girl" [@comcatholicgrl]). Importantly, the platform brought those in religious life into dialogue with laypeople online, where evangelization could happen instantly and around the clock. Organizations of religious whose charism incorporated the media, such as the Daughters of Saint Paul (@DaughterStPaul), gravitated toward the platform to establish ministries, as did those with a historical interest in science and technology, such as the Dominicans (@Dominican_Order). Individual priests have made good use of the platform for their own evangelization (e.g., Fr. Nicholas Rokitka, OFM Conv [@FrNickOFMConv], Fr. Cassidy Stinson [@thehappypriest], Fr. Harrison Ayre [@frharrison]), forming friendships and helping to shape the spiritual lives of thousands. The participants in this community are different from notable Catholic presences on Twitter like Pope Francis (@Pontifex) and Bishop Robert Barron (@BishopBarron) who command massive followings but only post (one presumes) through professional intermediaries and do not interactively engage online. In this Catholic community, the encounter with others through back-and-forth messaging is an essential attribute.

Another essential attribute of this community is the dialogue that forms around the ideas that circulate within it. Emerging Catholic writers such as Leah Libresco (@LeahLibresco), Matthew Walther (@matthewwalther), and Eve Tushnet (@evetushnet) have been able to parlay their posting into more conventional essay and book projects for mainstream Catholic and secular audiences, which in turn are widely discussed online. Twitter has also been a forum for the discussion of pieces from established Catholic magazines that now release material directly to the platform, such as *Commonweal* (@commonwealmag), *America* (@americamag), and *First Things* (@firstthingsmag), as well as more eclectic underground publications with strong social media roots, such as *The Lamp* (@thelampmagazine), *The Josias* (@josias_rex), and *New Polity* (@PostliberalTho1). Catholics of many different backgrounds, political orientations, and experiences with the church have been able to learn from one another and better appreciate their shared faith that provides a meaningful alternative to a purely secular life.

By the end of the last decade, the community had been dubbed "Weird Catholic Twitter" by the *New York Times*, with the journalist Tara Isabella Burton positively affirming that its members were "finding that ancient theology can better answer contemporary problems than any of the modern secular world's solutions."[1] The "Weird" part of the moniker stemmed from the combinations of ideas that were popular within the community but unexpected by secular critics (for instance, the belief in the literal resurrection of Jesus Christ and simultaneous rejection of the excesses of late capitalism). However, Burton also observed that the community had a membership drawn largely from the millennial generation and possessed only several hundred active posters who, even though they were seemingly online at all waking moments, had fairly limited reach in their evangelism. Further, excessive turbulence coming

---

[1] Tara Isabella Burton, "Christianity Gets Weird," *New York Times*, May 8, 2020, https://www.nytimes.com/2020/05/08/opinion/sunday/weird-christians.html.

from partisans within the community and trolls outside of it was a problem that reduced the amount of Catholic dialogue found on Twitter today. To understand why this turbulence appeared, one just needs to take a look at what Twitter was designed for and how it was implemented to support a very particular business model rooted in user engagement and advertising.

Think: Twitter was the product of a design effort in the period right before the smartphone was introduced. The platform was originally intended to accommodate microblogging in a form where users could post real-time updates about what they were doing, reading, or thinking at a particular moment in just 140 characters.[2] This was a novel idea back in 2007, as there was no way to quickly determine what people all over the globe were talking about: Twitter aggregated trending ideas in a single easily accessible place.[3] Users could follow each other and reply to posts, which let communities (like Weird Catholic Twitter) form organically as those with shared interests connected. In principle, the platform has not deviated much from this original design, only sporadically increasing the character count and adding new features over its nearly two decades of existence. However, some of those new features would be consequential to the continuing degradation of civility online. Importantly, there is no evidence that the software designers at Twitter attempted to anticipate any unintended consequences of their design choices when they implemented the platform.

Build: Twitter was built in a way that caused problems from the onset. Trending material was frequently sensational, obscene, or antisocial in nature. This is because users quickly discovered that they could increase engagement by publicly fighting with one another. Such bouts often began with a user baiting opponents with a post that contained a message designed to provoke angry

---

[2] Nick Bilton, *Hatching Twitter: A True Story of Money, Power, Friendship, and Betrayal* (New York: Penguin, 2014).

[3] Staley, "What Was Twitter, Anyway?"

replies, which was simultaneously controversial and disingenuous—users do not need to believe in what they are posting to provoke the intended response. Denizens of the platform became so conditioned to treating every conversation on Twitter as a heated debate that angry replies began to appear on the most innocuous of tweets.[4] This was a universal phenomenon, impacting all communities on the platform.

Instead of making a course correction, the company doubled down on features that facilitated attacks on anyone and everyone. For example, the quote-tweet feature (introduced in 2015), allowed a user to add their own text or images as a response to an existing post from somebody else, with both being shown to their own followers. This feature is widely used to mock others, as it puts the new content above the original message in a way that comes across as scolding when the new message is a response to the original.[5] It is now routine for users to chastise each other, even under seemingly nonsensical circumstances.[6] Why wasn't anything done to

---

[4] Consider an example that surfaced during the writing of this book. On August 27, 2023, on the feast day of St. Monica, Pope Francis posted this message to the @Pontifex account on Twitter: "Today we remember Saint Monica, mother of Saint Augustine: with her prayers and her tears, she asked the Lord for the conversion of her son! Let us pray for the many mothers who suffer when their children find themselves lost or on difficult paths in life." It was promptly greeted with this snarky reply from another user: "Her son was a drunken playboy who abandoned his own son to become a priest and doctor of the church who put guilt in the Catholic faith. The irony is he didn't feel guilty about abandoning his son. He felt guilty for stealing peaches when he was a teenager." See https://twitter.com/Pontifex/status/1695798325079843153?s=20.

[5] Staley, "What Was Twitter, Anyway?"

[6] Here is another example. On June 29, 2023, Cardinal Timothy Dolan, archbishop of New York (@CardinalDolan), encouraged Mass-goers to reconsider their attire in the following Tweet: "When we go to Mass, we should dress appropriately. I'm not talking about tuxedos, but we should clean up and have presentable dress. Let's restore, revive and maintain our reverence in the Most Holy Eucharist." It was subsequently quoted by a user on the platform with this text added above it: "& Don't forget to bring your wallet! There's a big 5th Avenue store INSIDE the worship space—as well as another gown [*sic*] the block." See https://twitter.com/CardinalDolan/status/1667532075371732995?s=20.

rein in such behavior? The answer is simple: Twitter is a business. More engagement means more advertising dollars flowing into the platform, as advertisers flock to where the users are. Thus the implementation of the platform prioritized making it a successful business above all else, regardless of its impact on society.

Do: Let's think about Twitter in the context of its Catholic user base, and how the community of Weird Catholic Twitter reflected some of the principles of Catholic Social Teaching, as laid out in the framework of chapter 4. As we pointed out above, at no point did the platform incorporate such principles in a conscious manner. Twitter is a case where three principles of Catholic Social Teaching emerged organically through the behavior of a specific group of users on the platform. *The Call to Family, Community, and Participation* is the strongest principle linked to Catholics on Twitter, as the platform was primarily used to create a virtual extension of existing groups that could plug newcomers into specific aspects of Catholicism, or the faith itself, for the first time. Twitter also serves as a forum for dialogue for a diverse church, connecting it to the principle of *Life and Dignity of the Human Person.* Finally, it became a place of *Solidarity* for users facing religious persecution in a secularizing world or ostracism within the faith for possessing certain political beliefs or sexual identities. And those directly engaged in service to the poor and marginalized were able to organize online, coordinating charitable giving and volunteer work.

The true value of the platform manifests when the above principles are adhered to, because they support authentic encounters with others. Writing about his own experience on Twitter, Fr. Nicholas Rokitka, OFM Conv, had this to say: "Most thankful for this platform and how it has helped me understand so many other peoples' situations in life. I'm certain it has made me a better minister, and I hope has led me farther down the path of holiness."[7] That the platform might lead one down the path of holiness is very

---

[7] Fr. Nicholas Rokitka, Twitter, July 30, 2023, 10:33 p.m., https://twitter.com/FrNickOFMConv/status/1685841049074176000?s=20.

much in line with Marshall McLuhan's original thinking on what information networks should provide users: a global village that fosters shared understanding, with an underlying spiritual basis.[8]

But all is not well on Catholic Twitter—we can find many places where the principles of Catholic Social Teaching have been violated. The community is encumbered by the same partisan political crisis that has infected society at large, which unnecessarily drives a wedge between people who otherwise would share much in common when it comes to their faith. This is particularly frustrating, since Catholicism isn't neatly situated within a single political orientation, nor could it ever be. Writing critically in the *National Catholic Reporter*, Mike Jordan Laskey has argued that "Catholic Twitter attracts those with the sharpest opinions and loudest voices like moths to a porch light."[9] Further, one finds an abundance of vanity projects and commercial activity that serves no real purpose other than to enrich the life of the content creator. This has plagued both secular and religious posters alike. In an interview conducted by *America*, Bishop Robert Barron questioned the underlying motivation of Catholic posters on Twitter when a lack of virtue is evident: "I believe that before someone presses the 'enter' button and posts something on social media, he or she should ask a simple question: 'Am I doing this out of love?' Love means, of course, willing the good of the other. If one is doing it out of hatred, or a desire for revenge or a need to impress one's friends, he should refrain from hitting that button."[10]

Where does Catholic Twitter stand today? The community, like the platform itself, is not what it was in its heyday. Prominent

---

[8] Ripatrazone, *Digital Communion*.

[9] Mike Laskey, "Hateful Things Flood Catholic Twitter Every Day. It's Still Worth Saving," *National Catholic Reporter*, October 24, 2019, https://www.ncronline.org/opinion/young-voices/hateful-things-flood-catholic-twitter-every-day-its-still-worth-saving.

[10] Sean Salai, "Bishop Barron: Catholic Twitter Could Learn a Lot from St. Thomas Aquinas," *America*, October 6, 2020, https://www.americamagazine.org/faith/2020/10/01/bishop-barron-interview-catholic-twitter-thomas-aquinas.

voices, such as Elizabeth Bruenig, have departed in response to the overheated political climate, and, anecdotally, we have observed that posting has declined in general while the above problems remain. This is a predictable outcome that any community on the platform can face, based on the software design choices made by the company in charge of it.[11] A more virtuous platform design, emphasizing the principle of *Subsidiarity*, would have helped substantially. The lowest level of control and the highest level necessary to maintain some semblance of order within the Catholic Twitter community would be that community itself. Interference from the company and parties external to the community could be mitigated through internal norm setting. To implement this would require a group membership facility, whereby group administrators would vet requests to join the community they are responsible for, thus limiting its size and restricting membership to those who are genuinely interested in participating in it in good faith. Such a mechanism is common in other social forums, such as mailing lists and Discord groups, but is not as prevalent on social media. This is an important lesson for future platform designers: do not exclude communities from the decision-making process and create more open platforms that can be readily adapted by anyone.

Case Study 2: Catholic Influencers on Instagram

Some Catholics have adopted Instagram as their platform of choice for pursuing faith online. The leaders of this community are Catholic influencers: Instagram users who have gained large followings by sharing content related to Catholicism. Influencers do not typically follow most of their followers in return, but may interact with them through question-and-answer sessions or when their followers comment on their content or send them a direct message.

---

[11] Staley, "What Was Twitter, Anyway?"

Accounts with large followings have been a part of Instagram from its start in 2010. In the early days, Instagram promoted exemplary accounts on the company blog, causing these accounts to gain massive followings.[12] Instagram users who desired fame and influence but weren't fortunate enough to make it on the blog quickly discovered alternative tactics to find more followers. By 2015, many highly followed Instagrammers began to receive brand deals to promote products on their accounts, earning them so much money they were able to quit their day jobs.[13]

Alongside influencers focused on things like fitness and fashion, Catholic influencers began to appear. Although it's hard to pinpoint exactly when Catholic influencing began, anecdotally speaking, many of the Catholic influencer accounts we (Louisa and Megan) follow started their accounts, or started posting Catholic content on their accounts, between 2016 and 2018. While most Catholic influencer accounts started as a genuine way to share the Gospel on an otherwise secular platform, we have observed that over time, some influencers have taken more questionable paths.

Catholic influencers have been accused of using the Gospel for profit[14] or self-promotion. While this has included excessive promotion of Catholic products, it has also involved products that do not have an explicit connection to the Catholic faith, like mascara or sandals.[15] *The Young Catholic Woman*, a popular blog, has criticized this phenomenon and decried the lack of authenticity and narcissism some Catholic influencers possess.[16] Further, some

---

[12] Frier, *No Filter*, 43, 140–43.

[13] Frier, 167, 168.

[14] Teresacmcnulty, "When Will We Realize Christianity Is Not for Sale?," Instagram, August 11, 2023, https://www.instagram.com/p/Cv02UDjLXcO/?img_index=1.

[15] Sabrina McCormack, "Why I Unfollowed You: An Open Letter to Catholic Influencers," *The Young Catholic Woman* (blog), April 12, 2022, https://www.theyoungcatholicwoman.com/archivescollection/why-i-unfollowed-you-an-open-letter-to-catholic-influencers.

[16] McCormack, "Why I Unfollowed You."

Catholic Instagram influencers have also promoted false teachings, which range from unambiguous heresy (e.g., arguing that Pope Francis is not the true pope) to less obvious but still incorrect teachings (e.g., arguing that merely being a good person leads to salvation). To better understand how these pitfalls arose, let's consider Instagram's Think → Build → Do sequence.

Think: Instagram's co-founders, Kevin Systrom and Mike Krieger, built the platform when they saw an opportunity to address multiple different pain points in the mobile photo sharing space, including the widespread frustration that photos taken with cellphone cameras were low quality and unattractive.[17] A formative moment from Systrom's undergraduate study abroad experience in Italy helped to inform their solution: a photography professor in Italy forced him to photograph with a low-quality camera, teaching Systrom to love imperfection and to appreciate that low-quality images can become art through editing.[18] This experience inspired Systrom to provide in-app image filters that turned low-quality mobile images into artistic expressions.[19] Although Instagram's image filtering has incited social critique for its detrimental effect on mental health,[20] early adopters of Instagram generally had a positive experience: "New Instagram users found that basic things, like street signs and flower bushes and cracks in the paint of walls, all of a sudden were worth paying attention to, in the name of creating interesting posts. The filters and square shape made all the photographs on Instagram feel immediately nostalgic, like old Polaroids, transforming moments into memories, giving people the opportunity to look back on what they'd done with their day and feel like it was beautiful."[21] The Instagram team wanted their

[17] Frier, *No Filter*, 19.

[18] Frier, 5.

[19] Frier, 23.

[20] Genesis Rivas, "The Mental Health Impacts of Beauty Filters on Social Media Shouldn't Be Ignored—Here's Why," *InStyle*, September 14, 2022, https://www.instyle.com/beauty/social-media-filters-mental-health.

[21] Frier, *No Filter*, 31.

platform to be a place where users could explore a world of interesting niches.[22] Importantly, the founders were decidedly against self-promotion and initially tried to suppress commercial activity on the app.[23] In the midst of all of this optimism, how did Instagram turn into a hotbed of inauthenticity, shameless self-promotion, and business ventures?

The founders weren't able to maintain the clarity of their vision forever, especially after Facebook (now Meta) bought Instagram in 2012.[24] Despite Mark Zuckerberg's promise that Instagram could operate independently, it ultimately became subject to internal pressure to conform to Facebook's goals, which centered around getting "as many people as possible to use Facebook as often as possible."[25] Although Instagram originally considered a number of different revenue models, including the addition of premium services,[26] the company ended up employing the advertising-based attention economy business model,[27] which forced it to maximize its user base and the amount of time those users spent on the app. As a result, growth and the competition for relevance against other social media apps like Vine, Snapchat, and Twitter began to take the platform in a new direction.[28]

Build: Instagram is first and foremost an app for sharing pictures, and the primacy of visual media on Instagram distinguishes it from other social media apps. The in-app filters were intended to satisfy the vision of the founders to allow users to transform low-quality smartphone photos into art. Rather than having a Facebook-like connection structure in which users mutually be-

---

[22] Frier, 81.

[23] Frier, 103, 82.

[24] Frier, 52.

[25] Frier, 55, 91.

[26] "Kevin Systrom and Mike Krieger, Founders of Instagram," *Inc.*, April 9, 2012, https://www.inc.com/30under30/2011/profile-kevin-systrom-mike-krieger -founders-instagram.html.

[27] Frier, *No Filter*, 118.

[28] Frier, 105, 110, 193, 195.

come "friends" with each other on the app, Instagram instead allows users to follow people they don't know. The founders intended this so that people could follow other accounts based on interest rather than on real-life friendship.[29] They chose to prominently display a user's follower and following counts to gamify the experience of using the app and to encourage users to keep coming back onto the app to check their stats.[30] The number of likes and comments is displayed when viewing posts.

As Instagram grew, the team strongly encouraged a particular style of posts they wanted on the platform: artistic and niche.[31] They did this by highlighting specific accounts in their e-newsletter and on the @instagram account that was accessible to all users. Although the founders initially resisted having advertising on Instagram, they eventually allowed it with one concession: advertising on Instagram would have to come off as genuine, akin to a visually pleasing post rather than an obvious ad.[32] Systrom made sure to train the app's biggest users and advertisers in the type of ad content he wanted to see on Instagram so they would set the tone for other users.[33] The founders of Instagram cared immensely about keeping the platform about creativity, design, and experiences rather than about obvious self-promotion.[34] However, as we'll soon see, this proved impossible.

Another key element of the app is the algorithm that determines the content users see and the order in which they see it. In the early days of Instagram, users saw the newest content from accounts they followed at the top of their feeds. But this setup didn't keep users as engaged with the app,[35] triggering a change in the algorithm that would focus it on the content itself. Instagram users

[29] Frier, 20.
[30] Frier, 20.
[31] Frier, 103.
[32] Frier, 118.
[33] Frier, 160.
[34] Frier, 83.
[35] Frier, 196–97.

organically discovered techniques for getting the updated algorithm to prioritize their posts, including creating visually stimulat-
ing content with reflective but optimistic captions and making
sure their posts received multiword comments soon after they
were posted.[36] What was intended to promote engagement on
the app thus also promoted inauthenticity and self-promotion.

Do: At its best, Catholic Instagram is a place of *Solidarity* for
like-minded Catholics. By following influencer accounts, Catholic
Instagram users are able to have spiritually enriching content in-
fused into an otherwise secular feed. In some cases, following
influencer accounts can help Catholics feel like they have a place
in the church. As a teen, Catholic blogger and Instagram influencer
Cecilia Pappas (@ceciliajeanblog) didn't feel like she fit in the
Catholic Church because, while she possessed deep faith, she was
otherwise a socially well-adjusted teen girl who liked fashion and
boys. She hopes her account can evangelize to girls with similar
interests in a relatable way, helping them to feel more at home in
the Catholic Church.[37] Though it's rare for a non-influencer to
catch the attention of an influencer (based on our observation of
these accounts), Catholic influencers do tend to befriend one another, forming strong faith-filled friendships that they wouldn't
have otherwise had. The one instance when non-influencers may
meet Catholic influencers is through influencer-hosted pilgrim-
ages, of which there have been many: Cecilia Pappas (@cecilia-
jeanblog) and Megan Wells (@megs__wells),[38] Claire Couche
(@findingphilothea),[39] and Sarah Hoyoung Ku (@asiancatholic-

[36] Frier, 233, 230.

[37] Cecilia Papas, "Growing Up in the Catholic Church, I Used to Feel like I
Never 'Fit In,'" Instagram, October 4, 2020, https://www.instagram.com/p
/CF7xUF-DGsD/?img_index=1.

[38] Cecilia Papas, "Nearly 40 Gals, Dressed in Pink & Orange, Galavanting in
Paris . . . Something I'll Never Forget," Instagram, June 28, 2023, https://www
.instagram.com/p/CuDK0nBPQsN/?img_index=1.

[39] Claire Couche, "Home! To Him! From the Moment I Told Mike I Had Been
Invited to Lead a Pilgrimage, He Was SO Encouraging and Joyful about It," Instagram, September 30, 2023, https://www.instagram.com/p/Cx1a2clrIKA/.

woman) and Meg Hunter-Kilmer (@mhunterkilmer)[40] are just a few of the Catholic influencers who have offered international pilgrimage experiences to their followers.

Another good fruit of Catholic Instagram is evangelization. (Although it's not one of the eight themes of Catholic Social Teaching we based our framework on, evangelization is an important related theme.[41]) Any time a Catholic with a public Instagram account posts faith-filled content, it has the potential to end up in the feed of a non-Catholic and evangelize them. An especially powerful example of this has occurred with attendees of Catholic Youth Summer Camp, run by Damascus Mission (@damascusmission). Damascus has put a lot of effort into marketing their ministries, especially Catholic Youth Summer Camp, through Instagram and TikTok. One of many good fruits from these efforts is that potential campers hear about Catholic Youth Summer Camp through social media, feel inspired to attend, and have powerful encounters with Christ while at camp.[42]

However, not all of Catholic Instagram is as positive. Systrom and Krieger really wanted Instagram to be a place of art and authenticity. They rejected commercialization and self-promotion. And yet, Instagram became a platform that is dominated by these things, even among Catholic users. How did this happen? While the founders provided good intentions to inform the app's design, other aspects of that same design got in the way.

Generally speaking, many of the app's problems stem from violations of the principle of *Subsidiarity*. One of our design principles within the theme of subsidiarity is to promote small groups rather

---

[40] Sarah Hoyoung Ku and Meg Hunter-Kilmer, "Share, Save, and Comment to Spread the Word! We Are Absolutely Thrilled to Be Offering This Pilgrimage to South Korea in September 2024," Instagram, September 14, 2023, https://www.instagram.com/p/CxLWkO4rWa6/.

[41] Pontifical Council for Justice and Peace, *Compendium of the Social Doctrine of the Church*, chap. 2.

[42] Damascus Mission, "This Is the Power of MEDIA and TESTIMONY. Blessed Carlo Acutis Pray for Us!," Reels, Instagram, July 19, 2023, https://www.instagram.com/reel/Cu41W4Zv_10/.

than large followings on social media apps when appropriate. The reason behind Instagram users being able to amass large followings was a reasonable one: the founders wanted people to follow one another based on shared interests. But a problem that surfaced was that while Instagram tried to set the tone for desired content by highlighting and promoting exemplary accounts, a rapidly growing user base made it difficult to encourage every user to post in that particular way—the company simply did not have the capacity to perform that sort of outreach.[43] The capability for users to have unlimited numbers of followers, along with the prominent display of the follower/following count that became a status symbol, opened the door for relentless self-promotion and subsequent commercialization.

We mentioned earlier that Catholic influencers have been criticized for their attitudes of authority. In one example of this, Catholic influencers will, at times, confidently spread heresy. While for some influencers this could stem from innocent mistakes, it would not be surprising to us if other influencers are stretching or sensationalizing ideas to gain more engagement with the Instagram algorithm in order to attain more followers—a common strategy also used by secular influencers. This problem could also be fixed by the principle of subsidiarity: if social media platforms prioritized small-group connection rather than growing as big of an audience as possible, there would be fewer opportunities for misinformed theological ideas to spread so quickly.

Catholic influencers have also been criticized for speaking with authority on topics that are not explicitly Catholic. *The Young Catholic Woman* blog that criticized Instagram influencers also noted that health, food, makeup, and fashion are some of the other topics Catholic influencers are providing dubious advice on.[44] The source of these strong opinions stems from the fact that Catholic influencers, like Instagram influencers of all stripes, have turned

---

[43] Frier, *No Filter*, 41.
[44] McCormack, "Why I Unfollowed You."

their accounts into commercial opportunities, accepting lucrative sponsorship and brand deals for a number of products, both faith-based and not.

Instagram's public metrics related to number of followers and number of likes and comments on posts led users to want to post content that would help them maximize these metrics to gain personal validation and social standing.[45] Over time, it became part of the culture of the platform to turn a large following into a business opportunity.[46] Of course, having a business is not necessarily a bad thing. Many small business owners have found success marketing on Instagram, which has led to more security for their businesses and their families. However, some of the tactics that have been used to find commercial success on Instagram have not been good.

In particular, digital marketing on Instagram can be performed in a way that is insidiously inauthentic. While influencers post their lives on Instagram in a way that is meant to look authentic, they may say or do things that are not actually authentic in order to sell a product.[47] It's an all too common experience when viewing the profiles of Catholic influencers to find them sharing deep and encouraging spiritual content, followed quickly by advertising for a product—even using that encouraging spiritual content to sell the product. We, the authors, have seen this most with Catholic influencers who are involved in multilevel marketing schemes, especially those focused around nontoxic beauty products like Beautycounter and Crunchi.

Viewed in the best light, some may say that this could be a way to help people see God in the everyday, to see the spiritual in the natural. While this may be true, for far too many Catholic Instagram users, this method of advertising comes off as frustratingly inauthentic. We can see that this manner of communicating does

---

[45] Frier, *No Filter*, 233.
[46] Frier, 170.
[47] Frier, 139.

not promote healthy dialogue. First, influencers are not entering the conversation with their authentic selves. Second, when they are engaging in theological conversations with the end goal of selling products, it erodes the trust they have built with their followers: did they have genuine belief in the inspiring content they shared about spirituality if they had a commercial goal in mind when sharing it?

Catholics must also be wary of adopting a consumeristic mindset,[48] which we are more prone to when being bombarded with advertisements on Instagram. It can become especially easy to rationalize a consumeristic mindset when we see other Catholics fostering consumerism. As we mentioned in the last chapter, not only is such a mindset bad for the soul, but it also props up a culture of superdevelopment for those in wealthy countries, which can have a negative impact on the poor and the natural environment. To the extent that Instagram influencers promote consumerism, they violate the *Life and Dignity of the Human Person* by encouraging behavior contrary to the spiritual life, the *Option for the Poor and Vulnerable* as increased consumption negatively impacts the poor (as we discussed in chapter 4), and *Care for God's Creation* as such consumption also negatively impacts the environment.

The Young Catholic Woman blog also criticized Catholic influencers for their lack of authenticity apparent in the deployment of hefty levels of curated and filtered content. This lack of authenticity is systemic throughout Instagram, as the ability of someone to have a large number of followers and ability to edit images both on and off the app contribute to the social pressure to post near perfect images. This is a double-edged sword. First, people want to post "Insta-worthy" images to gain an audience, and in fact, Instagram and its feed algorithm evolved to a point where it's impossible to grow an audience without editing images to some ex-

---

[48] William T. Cavanaugh, *Being Consumed: Economics and Christian Desire* (Grand Rapids, MI: William B. Eerdmans, 2008).

tent.[49] Such a large audience often coerces users into feeling more pressure to perform for their followers, which in turn encourages more edited and filtered content. In addition to the culture of editing images before posting that was fostered by Instagram's in-app filters, the ability for users to compete for follower counts was a systemic decision leading individuals to strive for unachievable perfection in their posts.[50] Again, we see that the principle of *Subsidiarity* would have helped here. If small-group connection was prioritized over growing an audience, there might have been less pressure to post aggressively filtered images, either to game the algorithm or to impress a large and impersonal following.

Case Study 3: The Buy Nothing Project

The Buy Nothing Project is an online movement that connects members of local communities together to give and receive items and services for free. It was founded in 2013 by two friends in Washington State, Liesl Clark and Rebecca Rockefeller, who were concerned about the disposable plastic items purchased by their neighbors ending up in the Puget Sound.[51] According to Buy Nothing's website, Buy Nothing "exist[s] to build resilient communities where our true wealth is the connections forged between neighbors."[52] Although Buy Nothing isn't explicitly Catholic, we have found that, at least in our local community of South Bend, Indiana, Catholics flock to Buy Nothing because of the way it effectively promotes many of the principles of Catholic Social Teaching. The idea of the gift economy, the economic philosophy behind Buy Nothing, is even included in the social teaching of the church

---

[49] Frier, *No Filter*, 173, 235.

[50] Frier, 163.

[51] Liesl Clark and Rebecca Rockefeller, *The Buy Nothing, Get Everything Plan: Discover the Joy of Spending Less, Sharing More, and Living Generously* (New York: Atria Books, 2021).

[52] "About Us," Buy Nothing Project, accessed October 19, 2023, https://buynothingproject.org/about.

94   *Virtue in Virtual Spaces*

in *Caritas in Veritate*. In that encyclical, Pope Benedict XVI notes that the human being is made for gift, and that incorporating an element of gratuitousness into economic systems will help them to become more authentically human (3). The Buy Nothing Project helps to foster the gift economy in local communities.

Think: The Buy Nothing Project clearly lists their guiding principles on their website, which we reproduce here in figure 5.1.[53] These principles direct all activities associated with Buy Nothing groups.

Buy Nothing Project Guide Principles

- We believe our hyper-local groups strengthen the social fabric of their communities, and ensure the health and vitality of each member.
- We come from a place of abundance—not scarcity.
- We believe in abundance, we give, we ask, we share, we lend and we express gratitude.
- We are a gift economy, not a charity. We see no difference between want and need, waste and treasure.
- We do not buy, sell, trade, barter, or otherwise exchange money for items for serviced.
- We measure wealth by the personal connections made and trust between people.
- We value people and their stories and narratives about the 'stuff.'
- We are inclusive at our core.
- We value honesty and integrity in all our interactions.
- We view all gifts as equal; the human connection is the value.
- We believe every community has the same wealth of generosity and abundance.

Figure 5.1. Guiding principles for the Buy Nothing Project as found on their website under "Buy Nothing 101."

Build: Through both Buy Nothing Facebook groups and groups on the dedicated Buy Nothing app, individuals can log on to their

---

[53] "About Us," Buy Nothing Project.

local community's group and offer to give away household items they no longer need, offer their services, or ask for a particular good or service that they need from their community. The key is that no payment can be charged or offered: everything given and received must be completely gratuitous. Each Buy Nothing group has a handful of trained moderators that ensure group members are participating according to the rules of Buy Nothing, including making sure that all items and services are given and received completely for free and that all conduct is respectful.

Do: Buy Nothing first and foremost exemplifies the *Call to Family, Community, and Participation.* Buy Nothing groups exist to strengthen communities. Through their existence, these groups enable members of various communities to connect and provide for one another in ways that may not have been otherwise possible. Buy Nothing groups are strict about who can be in them: a potential new member must indicate the neighborhood they live in to ensure they are actually a part of the community that the group is meant to serve. While rural areas may have one Buy Nothing group for multiple nearby towns, cities often have a Buy Nothing group per neighborhood. As of the time of the writing of this book, Buy Nothing has split South Bend into five communities by geographic proximity.[54] Although all five of these communities are in our city and thus we could easily travel to give and receive to anyone in any one of them, we may only join the community our neighborhood resides in. In this way, community among those who are physically closest to us is established through technological mediation.

Buy Nothing also supports the *Option for the Poor and Vulnerable.* Buy Nothing can drastically improve the lives of those who are housed but may be struggling to make ends meet. Receiving necessities for free can help community members stretch their budgets more effectively, and receiving other more "superfluous"

[54] "Find Your Community," Buy Nothing Project, accessed October 19, 2023, https://buynothingproject.org/find-a-group/?fbclid=IwAR1N_Uhwm8qxII7k1 n9V2kwgeFOgM0NqBN4AzPIyORJ9o3TpANUeelHus0c#rec479389413.

gifted items and services can help improve their quality of life and inherent sense of dignity.

Buy Nothing helps us to *Care for God's Creation.* Through giving away unwanted items as gifts and receiving secondhand items rather than buying new ones, Buy Nothing helps to reduce waste and keep excess items out of landfills.

Finally, Buy Nothing effectively embodies the principle of *Subsidiarity.* The design principles we proposed for subsidiarity include creating small-group technologies when appropriate, allowing users to self-direct the moderation of their sites, and creating smaller platforms for specific purposes. Buy Nothing lives out all of these principles to a T! By limiting participation in Buy Nothing groups to those who live in specific geographic areas, Buy Nothing forces their groups to be small. The moderators are members of the group themselves rather than external moderators. This gives the groups a sense of being self-regulated. At the same time, the moderators are trained by the Buy Nothing organization. This is a perfect example of subsidiarity being lived out at different levels: the moderation itself comes from the lowest level of participation, while the training comes from a higher level of participation to ensure its quality and standardization across all Buy Nothing groups. The Buy Nothing app follows the design principle of creating smaller platforms for specific purposes. Although the Buy Nothing Facebook groups exist within the greater Facebook (and the even greater Meta) ecosystem, the overlaying of particular rules of moderation to the group participants ensures that it is being used for its intended purpose.

Case Study 4: Hallow

Hallow is a popular meditation and prayer app used by Catholics. While not a social media platform, Hallow contains a number of community-oriented features that led us to examine it as a case in this book. The founders of Hallow wanted to write software to facilitate Catholic meditation after discovering contemplative prayer and *lectio divina* (a traditional monastic practice of reading, meditation, and prayer). They desired to create something that would function like secular meditation apps such as Headspace or Calm, but with a religious dimension. Prayer is at the center of the Hallow journey. Importantly, the founders acknowledged that their deep engagement with the Catholic faith began just shortly before forming the company, meaning the venture had a transcendent aspect for them.[55]

Think: Hallow, Inc. is structured as a public benefit corporation because the founders did not want to measure the company's success solely in financial terms. However, they are backed by venture capital (VC) funding.[56] The VC funding model requires rapid growth for the investors to see a significant return on their investment. Thus tension exists between the philosophy behind the app, the intention to facilitate the spiritual growth of users through the free and subsidized services provided, and the VC motivation to make a large return on an investment. Hallow is pursuing growth through a variety of avenues: increasing influencer engagement across multiple platforms, partnering with events like World Youth Day, expanding the languages of prayers to serve the global Catholic community, and more recently, introducing social features. But it remains to be seen how growth in the user base will translate into revenue or a lucrative acquisition by another company, and how the VC backers of Hallow will respond if financial targets are not met.

Before Hallow there were very few prayer apps, especially Catholic ones, and those apps focused on a simpler product. What Hallow introduced is a clean, elegant design that not only encourages users to interface with it over other apps but also provides

[55] "How It All Started—The Hallow Story," Hallow, accessed October 20, 2023, https://hallow.com/about/.

[56] Hallow, "Hallow App Crosses 10 Million Downloads, Tops App Store, and Closes $50 Million Series C Fundraise," PR Newswire, accessed August 28, 2023, https://www.prnewswire.com/news-releases/hallow-app-crosses-10-million-down loads-tops-app-store-and-closes-50-million-series-c-fundraise-301828490.html.

the foundation for a more comprehensive ecosystem through which new features, like community interaction, can be added with ease. The Hallow homepage clearly cites the intention to be an authentically Catholic app, with an advisory board stocked with vowed religious.[57] The company is setting out to bring practices of Catholic prayer into the twenty-first century through technological mediation. And there is a precedent for this: historically, Catholics have used the technology of their time to aid in worship. For instance, after the invention of the printing press, printed music began to be used as a worship aid. The Hallow app is merely the next iteration of this progression.

Build: At its core, the Hallow app combines audio recordings of prayer and other spiritual content with an easy-to-use user interface. While Hallow is known for its simple and clean-looking interface, the app has not reinvented the wheel—the design is inspired by existing meditation apps like Headspace and Calm that conform to the well-known Web 2.0 app style.[58] The use of familiar design patterns means that users can navigate quickly and easily through the app, allowing the experience of prayer, rather than frustrations with the interface, to command most of their attention.

Once the user clicks into a prayer or meditation, they are presented with customization options. Standard Catholic prayers like the rosary allow users to select from a number of different voice actor guides, including both Hallow employees and celebrity Catholics from Bishop Robert Barron to Mark Wahlberg. These prayer recordings generally have two to three options for how long the user wishes to pray, allowing for more or less time for silent contemplation amid the prayer. More recently, features have been added to support Mass-goers, such as the availability of the daily Mass readings in the app. While other apps, such as iBreviary, support this

[57] "How It All Started—The Hallow Story."

[58] Mary Farrow, "I Tried the Hallow App for Two Weeks and Here's How It Went," The Pillar, May 28, 2021, https://www.pillarcatholic.com/p/i-tried-the-hallow-app-for-two-weeks.

functionality, Hallow brings it into its sleeker and more intentionally designed platform. Hallow has also announced its intention to release an interactive community feature, with which users would be able to engage with members of their parish community in online fellowship. But as of this writing it has not debuted.

Hallow engages with the public through the use of influencers and celebrities who promote the app on social media and on television. A notable example of this is Mark Wahlberg's promotion of Hallow's #Pray40 Lenten Prayer Challenge. Wahlberg was used as a spokesperson on all major social media platforms (and even on some television shows like *The TODAY Show*) so excessively that Hallow's Lenten challenge (and humorously, the entire liturgical season of Lent) became known as *Mark Wahlberg's* 40 Day Prayer Challenge.[59] While he is the most prominent influencer for Hallow, Wahlberg isn't the only one. Many famous Catholic celebrities (and Christians from other denominations), influencers, and athletes have also participated in social media advertising for the app.[60]

The app keeps track of and displays to users the many thousands of people who have prayed particular prayers through it. This is similar to the follower counts or engagement counters found on other platforms, but Hallow channels user behavior into an endeavor that is wholly good in nature. Such counts cannot be exploited for commercial or self-indulgent purposes as similar counts are on Instagram and related platforms. It is possible for users to

[59] Kat Bair, "Mark Wahlberg's 40-Day Challenge," Ministry Incubators, February 28, 2023, https://ministryincubators.com/40-day-challenge/.

[60] Madeline Myers, "MOGL Announces NIL Partnership With Prayer App Hallow," *Business of College Sports* (blog), August 23, 2022, https://businessof collegesports.com/name-image-likeness/mogl-announces-nil-partnership-with-prayer-app-hallow/; Cate Von Dohlen, "Hallow's Athlete Partners: Prayers and Bible Verses for Sports," Hallow, August 22, 2022, https://hallow.com/blog /hallows-athlete-partners-prayers-and-bible-verses-for-sports/; Stephanie Palmeri, "You Gotta Have Faith . . . ," *Medium* (blog), April 19, 2021, https:// stephpalmeri.medium.com/you-gotta-have-faith-36c13d1dbc53.

track their praying streaks (*streaks* here refers to daily app engagements or habits), like most other prayer or meditation apps. Hallow has not yet functionalized the social aspect beyond daily shared prayers (called *dailies*) where users can see the number of users praying together. Even though it is not fully operational yet, Hallow does have an option for users to join a parish or retreat group.[61]

Do: This aforementioned feature that reports various prayer stats is especially visible in the "challenges" that Hallow continuously runs. The most famous of the Hallow challenges is, of course, the Lenten forty-day prayer challenge. However, Hallow has a number of other challenges throughout the year centered around novenas, spiritual writings, and other prayers and meditations fitting to the particular liturgical season. The company claims these challenges benefit the user through shared accountability, as one can view the total number of participants at any given time.[62]

The downside of this "challenge" approach to prayer is that it is a gamification of the prayer experience, whereby users track their streaks and are hyped up by seeing the thousands of other users signed up for their challenge. Challenges typically have fifty to one hundred thousand people praying together per challenge and reports of three hundred million or more prayers completed on the app. But how many of these prayers are genuine? It is possible that the audio recordings simply play while the user is off doing something else.

Concern could also be raised over the promotional use of celebrities like Mark Wahlberg, which may be leading some users to consider them to be Catholic authorities. However, these celebrities are able to persuade lay Catholics into the experience of daily prayer in a unique way. And one can argue that celebrity involvement in Hallow exposes their humanity. It is no secret that Mark Wahlberg isn't a perfect human (he has acknowledged participating in racially

---

[61] "Building Our Communities," Hallow, accessed October 20, 2023, https://hallow.com/communities/.

[62] Alex Jones, "54 Day Novena $10K Donation Challenge," Hallow, September 21, 2021, https://hallow.com/blog/54-day-novena-10k-donation-challenge/.

motivated assaults in Boston as a teenager[63]), but praying with someone who isn't perfect reminds us that prayer is for everyone.

As noted above, Hallow will soon support interactive social features, possibly making it more like conventional social media platforms. One concern is that this expanded social capacity naturally follows the acceptance of VC funding because investors expect an aggressive growth strategy for the business behind the app. But that need not be a problem if it doesn't undermine the vision of the founders. Growth in the Hallow user base is something we would like to see because it will help many people experience the Catholic faith for the first time or in a deeper way.

How does Hallow hold up in terms of Catholic Social Teaching? When it comes to the *Life and Dignity of the Human Person*, meditative prayer has a similar therapeutic benefit to other non-spiritual forms of meditation. But it is richer because it enables a relationship with our Creator, something that underpins the life and dignity of all of us. Similarly, the *Call to Family, Community, and Participation* happens through the app's promotion of prayer. How so? Although prayer through the Hallow app is usually an individual activity, prayer itself is a way to actively participate with the communion of saints and is the underpinning of a holy Catholic life that allows us to live well in community. Hallow also supports Catholic communities of learning by hosting the incredibly popular "Bible in a Year" and "Catechism in a Year" podcasts.[64] With respect to *Subsidiarity*, the first social features are being developed for parish and retreat communities. The idea of deeply integrating with local and in-person communities—the traditional level at which organized

[63] Michael Saunders, "Facing Protest, Wahlberg Apologizes for 'Racist' Action," *Boston Globe*, February 19, 1993, https://www.bostonglobe.com/metro /1993/02/19/facing-protest-wahlberg-apologizes-for-racist-action/C8QUpxt nexamtLjiSQIWxN/story.html.

[64] "Catechism in a Year Podcast with Fr. Mike Schmitz Launches on Hallow," Hallow, January 10, 2023, https://hallow.com/blog/catechism-in-a-year-fr-mike -schmitz/; "'Bible In a Year' Podcast with Fr. Mike Schmitz Now on Hallow," Hallow, accessed October 20, 2023, https://hallow.com/blog/bible-in-a-year -with-father-mike-schmitz/.

prayer has often been situated—is advanced through the app. This also stands in contrast to many secular social media platforms, which encourage unbounded social connection and virality.

But considering *The Dignity of Work and Rights of Workers*, Hallow may be walking on thin ice. On the surface, everything looks positive: recent job postings on the Hallow website advertise unlimited PTO, insurance, remote-flexible work, fully paid parental leave, 401(k) match, and stipends for health and wellness, home office, and learning.[65] While many of these benefits are in alignment with the dignity of workers, Hallow is still a venture-backed company. Coming back to the risks of the VC model of funding, growth in the business can lead to an environment that is not oriented toward the dignity of the workers, since scaling the business must coincide with increasing productivity. If more workers are hired, or if technological interventions make existing employees more productive without them spending more time at work, this can be managed effectively. If not, employees may be expected to work longer hours at the expense of family, friends, and other aspects of their personal life. The Public Benefit Corporation status of Hallow may prove to be a factor in the company avoiding this pitfall in the future. We also hope that the authentically Catholic mission of the company[66] overrides any poor business advice that may come from secular investors. Only time will tell.

What Did These Case Studies Teach Us?

While we should strive to conduct ourselves well on any social technology that we use, we see from these case studies that some apps make this easier than others through their design. Apps with intentional philosophies rooted in Catholic Social Teaching (even in cases like Buy Nothing where the founders likely did not realize their foundational philosophy was so connected to Catholic Social

---

[65] "Hallow Jobs," Lever, accessed October 20, 2023, https://jobs.lever.co/hallow.
[66] "Our Story," Hallow, accessed September 8, 2023, https://hallow.com/about/.

Teaching) and guardrails in their designs that help users stick to the intended behavior tend to foster the best experiences.

The focus on social technologies in this book was a natural choice because Catholic Social Teaching is concerned with how we live well in community, and there would be no communities without communication. However, Catholic Social Teaching can and should inform all types of technologies. In the next chapter we will apply our Catholic Social Teaching–based framework to generative AI to demonstrate its wider applicability.

Chapter SIX

Conclusion

Although we chose to focus on social technologies in this book, we can use Catholic Social Teaching to create frameworks to evaluate and guide the development of any type of digital technology. As we look toward the future, there are several technologies on the horizon that have revolutionary potential. Can we use Catholic Social Teaching to anticipate the challenges of these technologies or celebrate the good they will bring to society?

Generative AI and the Future of Social Technologies

One such future technology is generative artificial intelligence: intelligent systems capable of producing new text, images, audio, and other forms of data. Notable examples of generative AI include DALL-E,[1] which creates images from text prompts like "an oil pastel drawing of an annoyed cat in a spaceship" (figure 6.1), and ChatGPT,[2] a chatbot that allows for humanlike communication. ChatGPT (and its peers) can talk about a wide range of topics, answer questions, give advice, and even generate creative text, like writing stories or poems. It's kind of like having a virtual chat buddy that's always ready to chat and assist you with all sorts of things! These last two sentences

[1] https://openai.com/dall-e-2
[2] https://chat.openai.com/

were in fact generated by ChatGPT when we asked it to describe itself for a general audience. When technologies like DALL-E and ChatGPT were released to the public, they stirred up both awe and concern. Some worry that generative AI brings us closer to the AI singularity, a hypothetical future in which artificial intelligence agents surpass human intelligence.[3] Even though many artificial intelligence experts (including Walter, one of this book's authors) do not think that the singularity is something we need to worry about currently given the present state of AI research, generative AI still presents a number of unique benefits and dilemmas to society, which we can evaluate through the lens of Catholic Social Teaching.

Figure 6.1. An image generated by the DALL-E AI algorithm with the prompt "an oil pastel drawing of an annoyed cat in a spaceship."

[3] "Core Views on AI Safety: When, Why, What, and How," Anthropic, March 8, 2023, https://www.anthropic.com/index/core-views-on-ai-safety.

Evaluating Generative AI with Catholic Social Teaching

Several concerns with generative AI relate to the *Dignity of the Worker*. The advent of generative AI has caused concern that freelance writing and graphic design jobs will be put in jeopardy, as they can be easily replaced by platforms like ChatGPT and DALL-E.[4] However, generative AI may not put people out of their jobs entirely: some freelancers are now learning how to work in partnership with generative AI to have a competitive advantage in the marketplace.[5] Even so, generative AI algorithms have also come under fire for infringing upon the copyright of such creators. These algorithms work by learning patterns from massive amounts of data, including text and visual data. Creators whose intellectual property can be downloaded from the Internet are not fairly compensated for their work being used by tech companies to train AI algorithms. In defense of these companies, some say that this falls under the category of "fair use."[6] Even if it does, given the significant backlash emanating from the numerous content creators whose work has been used to train generative AI, it seems that their dignity should have been minded in this process and perhaps some compensation would have been appropriate.

Another concern is that generative AI will take away opportunities for people to express their creativity. Marissa Le Coz, a Catholic software engineer who writes about faith and technology on Substack, expresses the concern that generative AI may displace the human act of creation, which allows us to share in the *Imago Dei*.[7]

---

[4] Andrew Deck, "The Workers at the Frontlines of the AI Revolution," Rest of World, July 11, 2023, https://restofworld.org/2023/ai-revolution-outsourced -workers/.

[5] Deck, "Workers at the Frontlines of the AI Revolution."

[6] Alex Reisner, "Revealed: The Authors Whose Pirated Books Are Powering Generative AI," *The Atlantic*, August 19, 2023, https://www.theatlantic.com /technology/archive/2023/08/books3-ai-meta-llama-pirated-books/675063/.

[7] Marissa Le Coz, "The Imago Dei and Generative AI," Substack, September 24, 2023, https://theluddite technologist.substack.com/p/the-imago-dei-and -generative-ai?utm.

In her reflection, Le Coz echoes the thought of Pope John Paul II: in *Laborem Exercens* (5), he warns that technology can become man's enemy if it replaces him, taking away his personal satisfaction and his incentives for creativity and responsibility, rather than simply being a tool at the service of man's work.

However, in a piece that appeared in *Comment* magazine, one of the authors of this book (Walter) took a more hopeful view of generative AI, identifying it as simply a new artistic medium. He also observed that the "creativity" of generative art is constrained by the data the algorithm is trained with, so it will never be able to replicate all facets of human creativity. Thus, he hopes there will always be a place for human creativity in art. Walter also notes that elements of human creativity permeate all generative AI algorithms. In his words: "AI is a product of human ingenuity; thus, any AI necessarily carries with it some of the humanity that underpins creativity."[8] Generative AI will not necessarily violate our dignity as workers and creators as long as it is kept in its proper place rather than made an idol.

Another principle of Catholic Social Teaching that generative AI is at risk of violating is the *Option for the Poor and Vulnerable*. This violation is most apparent through the strategies OpenAI employed to build an offensive language detector to filter out troubling prompts. Although this tool has an important and positive societal impact, it caused collateral damage. OpenAI needed labeled examples of violence, hate speech, and sexual abuse to train the language detector to spot this data. They outsourced the labeling jobs to workers in Kenya, who were paid less than two dollars per hour and experienced severe mental distress from viewing so much explicit content.[9] We see here a vicious cycle: in order to

[8] Walter J. Scheirer, "The Human in AI," *Comment*, August 9, 2023, https://comment.org/the-human-in-ai/?utm.

[9] Billy Perrigo, "Exclusive: OpenAI Used Kenyan Workers on Less Than $2 Per Hour to Make ChatGPT Less Toxic," *Time*, January 18, 2023, https://time.com/6247678/openai-chatgpt-kenya-workers/.

prevent the general public from being vulnerable to toxic content on ChatGPT, OpenAI relied on a vulnerable population—workers in a poor country lacking better opportunities for employment—and made them vulnerable to mental distress through their task of reading explicit content all day.

In spite of the violations we just discussed, there are, on the other hand, use cases of generative AI algorithms that affirm the *Dignity of the Worker* and the *Option for the Poor and Vulnerable*. One such use case lies in the world of academia. In the present day, the *lingua franca* of the international research community is English. Researchers from all around the world must write in English in order to have their work published in the best venues. Recently, non-native-English-speaking scholars have found Chat-GPT to be an incredibly useful tool to assist in writing, including helping to correct grammatical mistakes and rephasing passages of text into more natural-sounding English. ChatGPT helps to affirm the dignity of non-English-speaking researchers (*Dignity of the Worker*) by allowing them to better communicate their research, and helps to make success in research more accessible to people who didn't happen to be fortunate enough to grow up as a native speaker of the research *lingua franca* (*Option for the Poor and Vulnerable*). However, it is important to note that while Chat-GPT can help more people write in English, using it for this purpose may further institutionalize English as the most important language. Language shapes how we think, and further emphasizing communication in English may subtly corral researchers to communicate in mimetic ways.

We've seen that generative AI can have positive and negative effects, even within the same theme of Catholic Social Teaching. Is there some way to limit the negative effects and promote the positive ones? We propose the principle of *Subsidiarity* as the solution, applying our suggestion to make smaller platforms for specific uses to generative AI systems. Consider Moveworks,[10] a platform that

---

[10] https://www.moveworks.com/.

brings a generative AI-powered chatbot into the workplace. Moveworks hopes to use conversational AI to help employees get answers to simple IT, HR, finance, and facilities questions. The company's website emphasizes that their conversational AI systems are not meant to replace IT, HR, finance, and facilities workers but rather to free up their time from answering simple questions so they have space to tackle more complex projects. No violation of the dignity of the worker is present in this use case if generative AI is limited to rote tasks and does not take on creative communication roles. Creativity in writing is a deeply human practice, one that shouldn't be taken away from people who enjoy it. Answering simple questions does not do this. The data used to train the algorithm specifically pertains to business productivity, so there are no concerns with infringing upon copyright or encountering offensive content. It seems like building a generative AI algorithm for a smaller, well-defined use case eliminates many of the social problems we find with more general generative AI applications.

David Chiang, a Catholic natural language processing (NLP) expert at the University of Notre Dame, agrees that generative AI has both good applications and aspects worthy of critique.[11] In terms of algorithms that generate language, he appreciates their positive applications but pointed out a few existential questions to ponder. First, people are increasingly using ChatGPT to compose emails and text messages. Does it affect our interpersonal communication when we communicate with an AI's words rather than our own? Additionally, ChatGPT can't be programmed to say something that is true, only to say something that is more likely to be said by a human. When humans say something, there is a relationship between the words they say and a concept in the world they are referring to. However when ChatGPT says something, there is no real relationship between the symbols (words) it outputs and the things those words refer to in the world. Here we see a significant epistemic and ethical difference: while we can *trust* human *testimony*, we can only *rely* on AI

---

[11] Louisa met with Dr. Chiang for a personal interview on October 2, 2023.

prediction. What are the implications of a system that can say something that is true when it has no actual concept of what truth is?

Ideally, we would like to build generative AI systems in a way that leverages their positive outcomes and minimizes their negative outcomes. Although all of the case studies in this book evaluated technologies in light of Catholic Social Teaching after they were built, Catholic Social Teaching can and should be used to guide the development of technologies before they are built. For example, if ChatGPT had been built with the *Option for the Poor and Vulnerable* in mind, perhaps the engineering team would have found a creative way to limit toxic content without subjecting already-marginalized people to mental trauma. More radically so, if Catholic Social Teaching always provided guiding principles for software, maybe generative AI as we know it wouldn't exist, but some other more ethical technology that we currently can't fathom would have been designed to meet the needs of non-native-English-speaking researchers needing to write coherent papers in English.

Summary

In his book *The Design of Everyday Things*, Don Norman, a seminal thinker in the areas of human-computer interaction, user experience, and design, shares that the most radical and innovative products come about not from incrementally enhancing what already exists but rather from reconsidering a user's root goals to inspire something completely new.[12] Rather than thinking about how we can "fix" social media or generative AI to better align with Catholic Social Teaching, we propose that we should rediscover our deeper goals and desires, whether that's connecting with friends or writing a research paper in a foreign language, and design completely new technologies to solve these problems—with Catholic Social Teaching in mind, of course.

---

[12] Don Norman, *The Design of Everyday Things*, rev. and exp. ed. (New York: Basic Books, 2013), 43.

Bibliography

AI Research Group for the Centre for Digital Culture. *Encountering Artificial Intelligence: Ethical and Anthropological Investigations.* Edited by Matthew J. Gaudet, Noreen Herzfeld, Paul Scherz, and Jordan J. Wales. Portland, OR: Pickwick Press, 2024.

Alford, Helen. "Virtue Ethics in the Catholic Tradition." In *Handbook of Virtue Ethics in Business and Management*, edited by Alejo José G. Sison, Gregory R. Beabout, and Ignacio Ferrero, 165–76. International Handbooks in Business Ethics. Dordrecht: Springer Netherlands, 2017.

Anderson, Monica, Emily A. Vogels, Andrew Perrin, and Lee Rainie. "Connection, Creativity and Drama: Teen Life on Social Media in 2022." Pew Research Center, November 16, 2022. https://www.pewresearch.org/internet/2022/11/16/connection-creativity-and-drama-teen-life-on-social-media-in-2022/.

Aswad, Evelyn. "Losing the Freedom to Be Human." *Columbia Human Rights Law Review* 52 (February 29, 2020).

Bair, Kat. "Mark Wahlberg's 40-Day Challenge." Ministry Incubators, February 28, 2023. https://ministryincubators.com/40-day-challenge/.

Baker, Peter C. "Hunting the Manosphere." *New York Times*, June 13, 2017. https://www.nytimes.com/2017/06/13/magazine/hunting-the-manosphere.html.

Baughan, Amanda, Justin Petelka, Catherine Jaekyung Yoo, Jack Lo, Shiyue Wang, Amulya Paramasivam, Ashley Zhou, and Alexis Hiniker. "Someone Is Wrong on the Internet: Having Hard Conversations in Online Spaces." *Proceedings of the ACM on Human-Computer Interaction* 5, no. CSCW1 (2021): 1–22.

Beatey, Katelyn. "Geek Theologian Kevin Kelly." *Christianity Today*, July 15, 2011. https://www.christianitytoday.com/ct/2011/julyweb-only /geektheologian.html.

Bilton, Nick. *Hatching Twitter: A True Story of Money, Power, Friendship, and Betrayal*. New York: Penguin, 2014.

Blaschko, Paul, Sam Kennedy, Wes Siscoe, and Chris Hedlin. "Training Manual." Sheedy Family Program in Economy, Enterprise, and Society Dialogue. University of Notre Dame, July 2022. https:// ethicsatwork.nd.edu/resources/dialogue-training-manual.

Bonner, Bo, and Brett Robinson. "Fall Conference 2022—Digital Temples of the Holy Ghost." De Nicola Center for Ethics and Culture, 2022. https://www.youtube.com/watch?v=CdeWXBGrByI.

Bowles, Cennydd. *Future Ethics*. East Sussex, UK: NowNext Press, 2018, chap. 3.

Burton, Tara Isabella. "Christianity Gets Weird." *New York Times*, May 8, 2020. https://www.nytimes.com/2020/05/08/opinion/sunday /weird-christians.html.

Buy Nothing Project. "About Us." Accessed October 19, 2023. https:// buynothingproject.org/about.

Catechism of the Catholic Church. 2nd ed. United States Catholic Conference —Libreria Editrice Vaticana, 1997.

Cavanaugh, William T. *Being Consumed: Economics and Christian Desire*. Grand Rapids, MI: William B. Eerdmans, 2008.

Center for Humane Technology. "The Attention Economy." Accessed August 3, 2023. https://www.humanetech.com/youth/the-attention -economy.

Chan, Darius K-S, and Grand H-L Cheng. "A Comparison of Offline and Online Friendship Qualities at Different Stages of Relationship Development." *Journal of Social and Personal Relationships* 21, no. 3 (2004): 305–20.

Chesney, Bobby, and Danielle Citron. "Deep Fakes: A Looming Challenge for Privacy, Democracy, and National Security." *California Law Review* 107 (2019): 1753.

Clark, Liesl, and Rebecca Rockefeller. *The Buy Nothing, Get Everything Plan: Discover the Joy of Spending Less, Sharing More, and Living Generously*. New York: Atria Books, 2021.

Clark, Meghan. "Subsidiarity Is a Two-Sided Coin." Catholic Moral Theology, March 8, 2012. https://catholicmoraltheology.com/subsidiarity-is-a -two-sided-coin/.

Cooper, Becky. "Why Is Chartreuse Hard to Find Right Now? Ask the Monks Who Make It." *New York Times*, April 14, 2023, sec. Food. https://www.nytimes.com/2023/04/14/dining/drinks/chartreuse -shortage.html.

"Core Views on AI Safety: When, Why, What, and How." Anthropic, March 8, 2023. https://www.anthropic.com/index/core-views-on-ai-safety.

Cross, Rachel. "The Metaverse: Environmental Costs of Virtual Reality." *Impakter*, June 1, 2022. https://impakter.com/the-metaverse -environmental-costs-of-virtual-reality/.

Das, Mehul Reuben. "PopeGPT: Pope Francis Releases 'The Vatican Handbook to Develop Ethical AI.'" Firstpost, July 3, 2023. https:// www.firstpost.com/tech/news-analysis/pope-francis-releases-the -vatican-handbook-to-develop-ethical-ai-12817132.html.

Deck, Andrew. "The Workers at the Frontlines of the AI Revolution." Rest of World, July 11, 2023. https://restofworld.org/2023/ai- revolution-outsourced-workers/.

Design Justice Network. "Design Justice Network Principles." 2018. https://designjustice.org/read-the-principles.

Douthat, Ross. *The Decadent Society: How We Became the Victims of Our Own Success*. New York: Simon and Schuster, 2020.

Dreher, Rod. *The Benedict Option: A Strategy for Christians in a Post- Christian Nation*. New York: Penguin, 2017.

Driscoll, Kevin. *The Modem World: A Prehistory of Social Media*. New Haven, CT: Yale University Press, 2022.

Farrow, Mary. "I Tried the Hallow App for Two Weeks and Here's How It Went." The Pillar, May 28, 2021. https://www.pillarcatholic.com /p/i-tried-the-hallow-app-for-two-weeks.

Frier, Sarah. *No Filter: The Inside Story of Instagram*. New York: Simon and Schuster, 2020.

Greer, Tanner. "The World That Twitter Never Made." The Scholar's Stage, July 15, 2022. https://scholars-stage.org/the-world-that-twitter -never-made/.

Gremillion, Joseph. "Medellin Documents." In *The Gospel of Peace and Justice: Catholic Social Teaching Since Pope John*. Maryknoll, NY: Orbis Books, 1976.

Hagey, Keach, and Jeff Horwitz. "Facebook Tried to Make Its Platform a Healthier Place. It Got Angrier Instead." *Wall Street Journal*, September 2021. https://www.wsj.com/articles/facebook-algorithm -change-zuckerberg-11631654215.

Haidt, Jonathan. "The Teen Mental Illness Epidemic Began Around 2012." Persuasion, February 8, 2023. https://www.persuasion.community /p/haidt-the-teen-mental-illness-epidemic.

Hallow. "'Bible In a Year' Podcast with Fr. Mike Schmitz Now on Hallow." Accessed October 20, 2023. https://hallow.com/blog/bible-in-a -year-with-father-mike-schmitz/.

Hallow. "Catechism in a Year Podcast with Fr. Mike Schmitz Launches on Hallow." January 10, 2023. https://hallow.com/blog/catechism -in-a-year-fr-mike-schmitz/;

Hallow. "Hallow App Crosses 10 Million Downloads, Tops App Store, and Closes $50 Million Series C Fundraise." PR Newswire. Accessed August 28, 2023. https://www.prnewswire.com/news-releases /hallow-app-crosses-10-million-downloads-tops-app-store-and -closes-50-million-series-c-fundraise-301828490.html.

Hallow. "How It All Started—The Hallow Story." Accessed October 20, 2023. https://hallow.com/about/.

"Hallow Jobs." Lever. Accessed October 20, 2023. https://jobs.lever.co /hallow.

Harwell, Drew, Taylor Lorenz, and Cat Zakrzewski. "Racist Tweets Quickly Surface after Musk Closes Twitter Deal." *Washington Post*, October 28, 2022. https://www.washingtonpost.com/technology /2022/10/28/musk-twitter-racist-posts/.

Heidegger, Martin, and William Lovitt. *The Question Concerning Technology*. New York: Harper & Row, 1977.

Hiniker, Alexis, and Jacob O. Wobbrock. "Reclaiming Attention: Christianity and HCI." *Interactions* 29, no. 4 (2022): 40–44.

Jasanoff, Sheila. *The Ethics of Invention: Technology and the Human Future*. 1st ed. Norton Global Ethics Series. New York: W.W. Norton, 2016, chap. 6.

Jones, Alex. "54 Day Novena $10K Donation Challenge." Hallow, September 21, 2021. https://hallow.com/blog/54-day-novena-10k-donation-challenge/.

Kawas, Saba, Jordan Sherry-Wagner, Nicole S. Kuhn, Sarah K. Chase, Brittany Bentley, Joshua J. Lawler, and Katie Davis. "NatureCollections: Can a Mobile Application Trigger Children's Interest in Nature?" *CSEDU* 1 (2020): 579–92.

Kesling, Ben. "Technology in Classrooms Doesn't Always Boost Education Results, OECD Says." *Wall Street Journal*, September 15, 2015. https://www.wsj.com/articles/technology-in-classrooms-doesnt-always-boost-education-results-oecd-says-1442343420.

"Kevin Systrom and Mike Krieger, Founders of Instagram." *Inc.*, April 9, 2012. https://www.inc.com/30under30/2011/profile-kevin-systrom-mike-krieger-founders-instagram.html.

Kwasniewski, Julian. "A Catholic Workspace." *Crisis Magazine*, August 12, 2023. https://crisismagazine.com/opinion/a-catholic-workspace.

Labbe, Mark. "Energy Consumption of AI Poses Environmental Problems." *SearchEnterpriseAI*, TechTarget, August 26, 2021. https://www.techtarget.com/searchenterpriseai/feature/Energy-consumption-of-AI-poses-environmental-problems;

LaFrance, Adrienne. "Trolls Are Winning the Internet, Technologists Say." *The Atlantic*, March 29, 2017. https://www.theatlantic.com/technology/archive/2017/03/guys-its-time-for-some-troll-theory/521046/.

Lagorio-Chafkin, Christine. *We Are the Nerds: The Birth and Tumultuous Life of Reddit, the Internet's Culture Laboratory*. Illustrated ed. New York: Hachette Books, 2018.

Lanigan, Tim. "Catholic Social Teaching: Subsidiarity." For Your Marriage. Accessed July 20, 2023. https://www.foryourmarriage.org/catholic-social-teaching-subsidiarity/.

Laskey, Mike. "Hateful Things Flood Catholic Twitter Every Day. It's Still Worth Saving." *National Catholic Reporter*, October 24, 2019. https://www.ncronline.org/opinion/young-voices/hateful-things-flood-catholic-twitter-every-day-its-still-worth-saving.

Le Coz, Marissa. "The Imago Dei and Generative AI." Substack, September 24, 2023. https://theludditetechnologist.substack.com/p/the-imago-dei-and-generative-ai?utm.

Libresco, Leah. *Building the Benedict Option: A Guide to Gathering Two or Three Together in His Name*. San Francisco: Ignatius Press, 2018.

"The Light Phone." Accessed July 6, 2023. https://www.thelightphone.com/.

Lyons, Dan. "In Silicon Valley, Working 9 to 5 Is for Losers." *New York Times*, August 31, 2017. https://www.nytimes.com/2017/08/31/opinion/sunday/silicon-valley-work-life-balance-.html.

MacIntyre, Alasdair. *After Virtue*. London: Bloomsbury, 2013.

Martin, Bruno. "The Hidden Environmental Toll of Smartphones." *OpenMind*, BBVA, February 24, 2020. https://www.bbvaopenmind.com/en/science/environment/the-hidden-environmental-toll-of-smartphones/.

McClain, Colleen, Emily A. Vogels, Andrew Perrin, Stella Sechopoulos, and Lee Rainie. "How the Internet and Technology Shaped Americans' Personal Experiences amid COVID-19." Pew Research Center: Internet, Science & Tech, April 2022. https://www.pewresearch.org/internet/2021/09/01/how-the-internet-and-technology-shaped-americans-personal-experiences-amid-covid-19/.

McCormack, Sabrina. "Why I Unfollowed You: An Open Letter to Catholic Influencers." *The Young Catholic Woman* (blog), April 12, 2022. https://www.theyoungcatholicwoman.com/archivescollection/why-i-unfollowed-you-an-open-letter-to-catholic-influencers.

McLuhan, Marshall. "The Electric Culture." *Renascence* 13, no. 4 (November 1, 1961): 219–20.

McLuhan, Marshall, and Quentin Fiore. *The Medium Is the Massage: An Inventory of Effects*. Richmond, CA: Gingko Press, 2001.

Melé, Domènec. "Virtues, Values, and Principles in Catholic Social Teaching." In *Handbook of Virtue Ethics in Business and Management*, edited by Alejo José G. Sison, Gregory R. Beabout, and Ignacio Ferrero, 153–64. International Handbooks in Business Ethics. Dordrecht: Springer Netherlands, 2017.

Mill, John Stuart. *Utilitarianism*. 2nd ed. Cambridge, MA: Hackett, 2001.

Miller, Ryan W. "What's 'Zoom Fatigue'? Here's Why Video Calls Can Be So Exhausting." *USA Today*, April 23, 2020. https://www.usatoday.com/story/news/nation/2020/04/23/zoom-fatigue-video-calls-coronavirus-can-make-us-tired-anxious/3010478001/.

Moretta, Tania, and Giulia Buodo. "The Relationship between Affective and Obsessive-Compulsive Symptoms in Internet Use Disorder." *Frontiers in Psychology* 12 (2021): 700518. https://doi.org/10.3389/fpsyg.2021.700518.

Myers, Madeline. "MOGL Announces NIL Partnership With Prayer App Hallow." *Business of College Sports* (blog), August 23, 2022. https://businessofcollegesports.com/name-image-likeness/mogl-announces-nil-partnership-with-prayer-app-hallow/.

Nix, Naomi. "Facebook Pivoted to the Metaverse. Now It Wants to Show off Its AI." *Washington Post*, May 14, 2023. https://www.washingtonpost.com/technology/2023/05/14/meta-generative-ai-metaverse/.

Norman, Don. *The Design of Everyday Things*. Revised and expanded ed. New York: Basic Books, 2013.

Palmeri, Stephanie. "You Gotta Have Faith . . ." *Medium* (blog), April 19, 2021. https://stephpalmeri.medium.com/you-gotta-have-faith-36c13d1dbc53.

Peñarredonda, José Luis. "What Happens When We Work Non-Stop." *BBC Worklife*, August 23, 2018. https://www.bbc.com/worklife/article/20180823-how-bad-for-you-is-working-non-stop.

Perrigo, Billy. "Exclusive: OpenAI Used Kenyan Workers on Less Than $2 Per Hour to Make ChatGPT Less Toxic." *Time*, January 18, 2023. https://time.com/6247678/openai-chatgpt-kenya-workers/.

Pontifical Council for Justice and Peace. *Compendium of the Social Doctrine of the Church*. Washington, DC: USCCB Publishing, 2005.

Pope Benedict XVI. "43rd World Communications Day—New Technologies, New Relationships. Promoting a Culture of Respect, Dialogue and Friendship," May 24, 2009. https://www.vatican.va/content/benedict-xvi/en/messages/communications/documents/hf_ben-xvi_mes_20090124_43rd-world-communications-day.html.

Pope Benedict XVI. "47th World Communications Day—Social Networks: Portals of Truth and Faith; New Spaces for Evangelization," May 12, 2013. https://www.vatican.va/content/benedict-xvi /en/messages/communications/documents/hf_ben-xvi_mes _20130124_47th-world-communications-day.html.

Pope Benedict XVI. *Caritas in Veritate.* Vatican, June 29, 2009. https:// www.vatican.va/content/benedict-xvi/en/encyclicals/documents /hf_ben-xvi_enc_20090629_caritas-in-veritate.html.

Pope Francis. *Evangelii Gaudium.* Vatican, November 24, 2013. https://www .vatican.va/content/francesco/en/apost_exhortations/documents /papa-francesco_esortazione-ap_20131124_evangelii-gaudium.html.

Pope Francis. *Fratelli Tutti.* Vatican, October 3, 2020. https://www .vatican.va/content/francesco/en/encyclicals/documents/papa -francesco_20201003_enciclica-fratelli-tutti.html.

Pope Francis. *Humanam Progressionem.* Vatican, August 17, 2016. https:// www.vatican.va/content/francesco/en/motu_proprio/documents /papa-francesco-motu-proprio_20160817_humanam-progressionem .html.

Pope Francis. *Laudato Si '.* Vatican, May 24, 2015. https://www.vatican .va/content/francesco/en/encyclicals/documents/papa-francesco _20150524_enciclica-laudato-si.html.

Pope Francis. "Message for the 2014 World Communications Day (January 24, 2014)." *AAS* 106 (2014): 113.

Pope Francis. "Video Message to the TED Conference in Vancouver." *L'Osservatore Romano* (April 26, 2017): 7.

Pope John XXIII. *Mater et Magistra.* Vatican, May 15, 1961. https://www .vatican.va/content/john-xxiii/en/encyclicals/documents/hf_j-xxiii _enc_15051961_mater.html.

Pope John XXIII. *Pacem in Terris.* Vatican, April 11, 1963. https://www .vatican.va/content/john-xxiii/en/encyclicals/documents/hf_j-xxiii _enc_11041963_pacem.html.

Pope John Paul II. "36th World Communications Day—Internet: A New Forum for Proclaiming the Gospel," May 12, 2002. https://www .vatican.va/content/john-paul-ii/en/messages/communications /documents/hf_jp-ii_mes_20020122_world-communications-day .html.

Pope John Paul II. "39th World Communications Day—The Communications Media: At the Service of Understanding among Peoples," May 8, 2005. https://www.vatican.va/content/john-paul-ii/en /messages/communications/documents/hf_jp-ii_mes_20050124 _world-communications-day.html.

Pope John Paul II. *Centesimus Annus.* Vatican, May 1, 1991. https://www .vatican.va/content/john-paul-ii/en/encyclicals/documents/hf_jp -ii_enc_01051991_centesimus-annus.html.

Pope John Paul II. *Laborem Exercens.* Vatican, September 14, 1981. https://www.vatican.va/content/john-paul-ii/en/encyclicals /documents/hf_jp-ii_enc_14091981_laborem-exercens.html.

Pope John Paul II. *Sollicitudo Rei Socialis.* Vatican, December 30, 1987. https://www.vatican.va/content/john-paul-ii/en/encyclicals /documents/hf_jp-ii_enc_30121987_sollicitudo-rei-socialis.html.

Pope Leo XIII. *Rerum Novarum.* Vatican, 1891. https://www.vatican .va/content/leo-xiii/en/encyclicals/documents/hf_l-xiii_enc _15051891_rerum-novarum.html.

Pope Paul VI. *Evangelii Nuntiandi.* Vatican, December 8, 1975. https:// www.vatican.va/content/paul-vi/en/apost_exhortations /documents/hf_p-vi_exh_19751208_evangelii-nuntiandi.html.

Pope Paul VI. *Gaudium et Spes.* December 7, 1965. In *Vatican Council II: Constitutions, Decrees, Declarations; The Basic Sixteen Documents*, edited by Austin Flannery. Collegeville, MN: Liturgical Press, 2014.

Pope Paul VI. *Inter Mirifica.* Vatican, December 4, 1963. https://www .vatican.va/archive/hist_councils/ii_vatican_council/documents /vat-ii_decree_19631204_inter-mirifica_en.html.

Pope Paul VI. *Populorum Progressio.* Vatican, March 26, 1967. https:// www.vatican.va/content/paul-vi/en/encyclicals/documents/hf_p -vi_enc_26031967_populorum.html.

Reich, Rob, Mehran Sahami, and Jeremy M. Weinstein. *System Error: Where Big Tech Went Wrong and How We Can Reboot.* New York: HarperCollins, 2021.

Reiner, J. Toby. "New Directions in Just-War Theory." *Monographs, Books, and Publications* 397 (July 30, 2018). https://press.armywarcollege .edu/monographs/397.

Reisner, Alex. "Revealed: The Authors Whose Pirated Books Are Powering Generative AI." *The Atlantic*, August 19, 2023. https://www.theatlantic.com/technology/archive/2023/08/books3-ai-meta-llama-pirated-books/675063/.

Ripatrazone, Nick. *Digital Communion: Marshall McLuhan's Spiritual Vision for a Virtual Age.* Minneapolis: Augsburg Fortress, 2022.

Rivas, Genesis. "The Mental Health Impacts of Beauty Filters on Social Media Shouldn't Be Ignored—Here's Why." *InStyle*, September 14, 2022. https://www.instyle.com/beauty/social-media-filters-mental-health.

Ruggeri, Amanda. "The Compelling Case for Working a Lot Less." *BBC Worklife*, December 4, 2017. https://www.bbc.com/worklife/article/20171204-the-compelling-case-for-working-a-lot-less.

Salai, Sean. "Bishop Barron: Catholic Twitter Could Learn a Lot from St. Thomas Aquinas." *America*, October 6, 2020. https://www.americamagazine.org/faith/2020/10/01/bishop-barron-interview-catholic-twitter-thomas-aquinas.

Samuel, Sigal. "It's Hard to Be a Moral Person. Technology Is Making It Harder." Vox, July 27, 2021. https://www.vox.com/the-highlight/22585287/technology-smartphones-gmail-attention-morality.

Saunders, Michael. "Facing Protest, Wahlberg Apologizes for 'Racist' Action." *Boston Globe*, February 19, 1993. https://www.bostonglobe.com/metro/1993/02/19/facing-protest-wahlberg-apologizes-for-racist-action/C8QUpxtnexamtLjiSQIWxN/story.html.

Scanlon, Krystal. "BeReal Still Has Potential for Advertisers, but Its Hype Period Is Well and Truly Over." Digiday, February 28, 2023. https://digiday.com/marketing/bereal-still-has-potential-for-advertisers-but-its-hype-period-is-well-and-truly-over/.

Scheirer, Walter J. "The Human in AI." *Comment*, August 9, 2023. https://comment.org/the-human-in-ai/?utm.

Sedmak, Clemens, and Kelli Reagan Hickey. *Counting the Cost: Financial Decision-Making, Discipleship, and Christian Living.* Enacting Catholic Social Tradition. Collegeville, MN: Liturgical Press, 2023.

Sgreccia, Elio. *Personalist Bioethics: Foundations and Applications.* Philadelphia: National Catholic Bioethics Center, 2012.

Smith, Noah. "Interview: Kevin Kelly, Editor, Author, and Futurist." *Noahpinion* (blog), March 7, 2023. https://www.noahpinion.blog/p /interview-kevin-kelly-editor-author.

Smith, Noah. "The New 1970s." *Noahpinion* (blog), July 24, 2023. https:// www.noahpinion.blog/p/the-new-1970s.

Staley, Willy. "What Was Twitter, Anyway?" *New York Times*, April 18, 2023, sec. Magazine. https://www.nytimes.com/2023/04/18/magazine /twitter-dying.html.

Taylor, Charles. *The Ethics of Authenticity*. Cambridge, MA: Harvard University Press, 2018.

Thompson, Derek. "Workism Is Making Americans Miserable." *The Atlantic*, February 24, 2019. https://www.theatlantic.com/ideas /archive/2019/02/religion-workism-making-americans-miserable /583441/.

Toyama, Kentaro. *Geek Heresy*. New York: PublicAffairs, 2015.

United States Conference of Catholic Bishops. "Civilize It: Loving Our Neighbor through Dialogue | Amar a Nuestro Vecino a Través Del Diálogo." USCCB. Accessed August 4, 2023. https://www.usccb .org/resources/civilize-it-loving-our-neighbor-through-dialogue -amar-nuestro-vecino-traves-del-dialogo.

United States Conference of Catholic Bishops. "Loving Our Neighbor through Dialogue." USCCB, 2021. https://www.usccb.org/resources /Loving-our-Neighbor-through-Dialogue.pdf.

United States Conference of Catholic Bishops. "Seven Themes of Catholic Social Teaching." USCCB, 2003. https://www.usccb.org/beliefs -and-teachings/what-we-believe/catholic-social-teaching/seven -themes-of-catholic-social-teaching.

U.S. Surgeon General. "Social Media and Youth Mental Health." U.S. Department of Health and Human Services, 2023. https://www .hhs.gov/surgeongeneral/priorities/youth-mental-health/social -media/index.html.

Vallor, Shannon. *Technology and the Virtues: A Philosophical Guide to a Future Worth Wanting*. New York: Oxford University Press, 2016.

Verbeek, Peter-Paul. *Moralizing Technology: Understanding and Designing the Morality of Things.* Chicago: University of Chicago Press, 2011. https://press.uchicago.edu/ucp/books/book/chicago/M/bo11309162.html.

Von Dohlen, Cate. "Hallow's Athlete Partners: Prayers and Bible Verses for Sports." Hallow, August 22, 2022. https://hallow.com/blog/hallows-athlete-partners-prayers-and-bible-verses-for-sports/.

Waldstein, Edmund. "The Eucharist in the Plan of Salvation, First Part." *Sancrucensis* (blog), March 19, 2023. https://sancrucensis.wordpress.com/2023/03/19/the-eucharist-in-the-plan-of-salvation-first-part/.

Wu, Carole-Jean, Ramya Raghavendra, Udit Gupta, Bilge Acun, Newsha Ardalani, Kiwan Maeng, Gloria Chang, et al. "Sustainable AI: Environmental Implications, Challenges and Opportunities." *Proceedings of Machine Learning and Systems* 4 (2022): 795–813.

Yuan, Shupei, Syed Ali Hussain, Kayla D. Hales, and Shelia R. Cotten. "What Do They Like? Communication Preferences and Patterns of Older Adults in the United States: The Role of Technology." *Educational Gerontology* 42, no. 3 (October 2015).

Zuboff, Shoshana. "Big Other: Surveillance Capitalism and the Prospects of an Information Civilization." *Journal of Information Technology* 30, no. 1 (2015): 75–89.

Milton Keynes UK
Ingram Content Group UK Ltd.
UKHW021844190924
448478UK00010B/208

9 798400 800269